D0443492

ALSO BY ANNE FADIMAN

The Spirit Catches You and You Fall Down

Ex Libris

At Large and At Small

EDITED BY ANNE FADIMAN

The Best American Essays 2003

Rereadings

The Wine Lover's Daughter

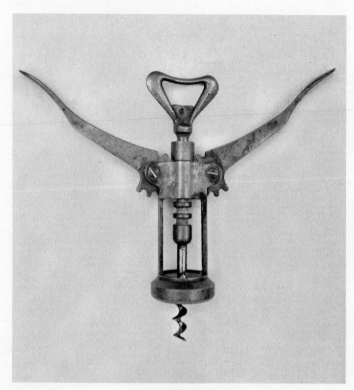

My father's corkscrew

The

Wine Lover's Daughter

A MEMOIR

Anne Fadiman

Farrar, Straus and Giroux

New York

Farrar, Straus and Giroux
18 West 18th Street, New York 10011

Portions of this book originally appeared, in slightly different form,
on newyorker.com and in *The Yale Review*.

Extract from Ernest Hemingway's letter on page 106 published with the
permission of The Ernest Hemingway Foundation, copyright © 2017.

Photograph credits appear on page 257.

Library of Congress Cataloging-in-Publication Data
Names: Fadiman, Anne, 1953– author.
Title: The wine lover's daughter : a memoir / Anne Fadiman.
Description: First edition. | New York : Farrar, Straus and Giroux, 2017. |
   Includes bibliographical references.
Identifiers: LCCN 2017008723 | ISBN 9780374228088 (hardcover) |
   ISBN 9780374711764 (ebook)
Subjects: LCSH: Fadiman, Anne, 1953—Family. | Women journalists—
   United States—Biography. | Fathers and daughters—Biography. |
   Fadiman, Clifton, 1904–1999. | Intellectuals—United States—
   Biography. | Authors—United States—Biography. | Editors—United
   States—Biography. | Wine and wine making—Miscellanea.
Classification: LCC PS3556.A314 Z46 2017 | DDC 813/.54 [B] —dc23
LC record available at https://lccn.loc.gov/2017008723

Our books may be purchased in bulk for promotional, educational,
or business use. Please contact your local bookseller or the Macmillan
Corporate and Premium Sales Department at 1-800-221-7945, extension
5442, or by e-mail at MacmillanSpecialMarkets@macmillan.com.

www.fsgbooks.com
www.twitter.com/fsgbooks • www.facebook.com/fsgbooks

1   3   5   7   9   10   8   6   4   2

For Susannah Fadiman Colt
and
Henry Clifton Fadiman Colt

Contents

The Wine Lover's Daughter

1

Thwick

My father was a lousy driver and a two-finger typist, but he could open a wine bottle as deftly as any swain ever undressed his lover. Nearly every evening of my childhood, I watched him cut the capsule—the foil sleeve that sheathes the bottleneck—with a sharp knife. Then he plunged the bore of a butterfly corkscrew into the exact center of the cork, twirled the handle, and, after the brass levers rose like two supplicant arms, pushed them down and gently twisted out the cork. Its pop was satisfying but restrained, not the fustian *whoop* of a champagne cork but a well-bred *thwick*. He once said that the cork was one of three inventions that had proved unequivocally beneficial to the human race. (The others were the wheel and Kleenex.)

If the wine was old, he poured it into a crystal decanter, slowing at the finish to make sure the sediment stayed in the bottle. If it was young, he set the bottle in a napkin-swathed silver cradle to "breathe": one of several words, along with "nose" and "legs" and "full-bodied," that made wine sound more like a person than a thing. Our food was served—looking back, I can hardly believe I once accepted this as a matter of course—by a uniformed cook who ate alone in the kitchen and was summoned by an electric bell screwed to the underside of the dinner table just above my mother's right knee. But my father always poured the wine himself. The glasses were clear and thin-stemmed, their bowls round and generous for reds, narrow and upright for whites. (Had he lived long enough to see *Sideways*, he would immediately have recognized that the wine-snob hero was seriously depressed: only thoughts of suicide could drive someone to drink a Cheval Blanc '61 from a Styrofoam cup.) He swirled the wine, sniffed it, sipped it, swished it, and, ecstatically narrowing his eyes, swallowed it—a swallow that, as he put it, led "a triple life: one in the mouth, another in the course of slipping down the gullet, still another, a beautiful ghost, the moment afterward."

My father, Clifton Fadiman, was a writer, and that erotically charged description is from a 1957 essay called "Brief History of a Love Affair." When I was ten or so, I spotted the title in the table of contents in one of his books, eagerly flipped to page 133, and was grievously disappointed to discover, in the fourth paragraph, that the lover in question was not a woman but a liquid.

That essay contained a number of words (including "sybaritic," "connubial," and "consummation") whose meanings I didn't know but that I enjoyed attempting to puzzle out. Ours was a word-oriented family. My father once wrote a children's book, based on bedtime stories he'd told my brother and me, about Wally the Word-worm, a small, hungry, bibliophilic invertebrate in a red baseball cap who, unsatisfied by the "short, flat, bare, dull, poor, thin" words he found in picture books, bliss-fully ate his way through a dictionary from "abracadabra" to "zymurgy." Along with Wally, my brother and I were fed a steady diet of polysyllables, of which wine provided some of the best-tasting. For instance: Rehoboam, Me-thuselah, Balthazar, and Nebuchadnezzar (giant wine bottles with, respectively, six, eight, sixteen, and twenty times the standard capacity) and Auslese, Beerenauslese, and Trockenbeerenauslese (three incrementally recher-ché German dessert wines made from ripe, very ripe, and very very ripe grapes). By the sixth grade, I would have recognized the names of all four *Premier Cru* Bordeaux—Château Latour, Château Margaux, Château Haut-Brion, and Château Lafite Rothschild—plus Château Mouton Rothschild, which wouldn't be elevated from second- to first-growth status until I was twenty. Plus some of the *Grand Cru* Burgundies: Chambertin, Montrachet, La Tâche, Grands Échézeaux, Romanée-Conti. Plus twenty or thirty other oenological terms, including Madeira, Marsala, Riesling, Rhône, Sauternes, sherry, port, claret, vermouth, aperitif, bouquet, phylloxera, *pourriture noble*, *vin ordinaire*, *doux*, *sec*, *demi-sec*, and *pétillant*. Some were murky but recognizable, like unmet second cousins whose names I'd overheard at the dinner table. Others were so familiar that I felt I'd always known them, just as I'd always known that white wines were really yellow and red wines were really maroon (though I couldn't have told you the first thing about rosés, which my father considered sissyish and never served). I knew that the great years—rather, the Great Years, since the phrase sounded so magnificent that I mentally capitalized it—were mostly odd numbers. I could have recited several: '29, '45, '49, '59.

My father wasn't exactly Jack Hemingway, who drank Château Margaux with his wife on the night his daughter Margot was conceived (she changed her name to Margaux after she heard the story), or Robert Lescher, my first literary agent, who once dipped his finger in a glass of Château d'Yquem '29, a Great Year from the greatest of all Sauternes, and placed a drop on the tongue of his six-week-old daughter (she smiled). However, starting when my brother and I were about ten, he regularly offered us watered wine, or, rather, wined water. I hated it but assumed that puberty would grant me a taste for Châteauneuf-du-Pape, along with a taste for French kissing and all the other things that ten-year-olds found disgusting but adults reportedly enjoyed. It was a foregone conclusion that I would love wine some day. I wouldn't be my father's daughter if I didn't.

2

Civilization

I never heard my father describe a wine as frisky or foxy or shy or insouciant, or say it had an oaky nose or a flinty finish or notes of pomegranate or the slightest soupçon of chanterelle. He didn't call Burgundy a Pindaric dithyramb (like George Meredith) or remark that drinking Dom Pérignon '53 above the temperature of 38 degrees Fahrenheit was simply not done (like James Bond). He made fun of the kind of snob who claimed he could discern, from a few bravura sips, which side of the hill the grapes had grown on. He frowned on patrons of expensive restaurants who sent bottles back to the kitchen just to prove they were somebodies. He wrote about wine, judged wine contests, supplied introductions to wine catalogs, invested in a wine-importing firm, and owned a first edition of the *Encyclopædia of Wines and Spirits* (a volume that has since passed to me, along with the rest of his wine library) inscribed by its author, Alexis Lichine, to "Kip, whose knowledge of the contents of this book is greater than its 730 pages." Nonetheless, he claimed he was not a bona fide connoisseur, merely a wine lover.

Because my father was unambiguously heterosexual, the object of his affections was invariably feminine. She might be "a country-wench Rhône, surrendering at once its all"; she might be a Chassagne-Montrachet '45, of which he drank an entire bottle, accompanied by two cans of unheated Vienna sausages, when he "ravished" the kitchen at 3:00 a.m. after writing for most of the night. The amorous vocabulary wasn't a metaphor. Aside from books, he loved nothing—and no one—longer, more ardently, or more faithfully than he loved wine.

These were some of his reasons.

Wine provided sensory pleasures equaled only by sex.

Wine was complex. "Water and milk," he wrote, "may be excellent drinks, but their charms are repetitive. God granted them swallowability, and rested."

Wine was various, both in its chemistry (alcoholic content, sugar, iron, tannins) and in its moods (champagne for celebration, port for consolation).

Wine was companionable. "A bottle of wine begs to be shared," he wrote. "I have never met a miserly wine lover."

Wine was hierarchical. One of my father's favorite adjectives—whether applied to wines, cheeses, or minds— was "first-rate," with the unspoken implication that below it, tier upon tier upon tier, were arrayed the second-rate, the third-rate, and the tenth-rate. There were no visible rankings on the labels of American wines, which

were based on grape varieties, but a French bottle pro-
claimed its contents' social station, from the blue-blooded
Appellation d'Origine Contrôlée (which included *Grand
Cru* and *Premier Cru*), through *Vin Délimité de Qualité
Supérieure*, all the way down to the humble *Vin de Pays*
and the still humbler *Vin de Table*. Although he disliked
wine snobs, my father harbored an even keener dislike
for what he called "wine *sans-culottes*." (He assumed his
readers would know that a *sans-culotte* was a lower-class
republican in the French Revolution. Politically speaking,
he supported the revolutionaries; culturally speaking, he
was aligned with those who got their heads chopped off.)
A wine *sans-culotte* was opposed to pecking orders and
thus rejected the fact that some wines were better than
others in favor of the dangerous fallacy that a good wine
was whatever wine you liked.

Wine was a *subject*—what Arnold Toynbee called
"an intelligible field of study." If you had a first-rate mind,
you could learn how wine was made, how to distinguish
one wine from another, how to pronounce their names,
and ten thousand other little pieces of knowledge that fit-
ted together to form an aesthetically pleasing whole. The
very act of drinking wine was an intellectual exercise. "I
know no other liquid," wrote my father, "that, placed in
the mouth, forces one to think."

Wine was not vulgar. My father believed that many
aspects of contemporary American life *were* vulgar, including bubblegum; waitresses who used "au jus" as a
noun instead of a prepositional phrase; self-help books,
which, because they bore no relation to real books and

My father with two of his favorite things: a cigar and a new shipment of wine, 1984

every relation to deodorants and laxatives, should, in his opinion, be called "word products"; off-rhymes in advertising jingles ("time" with "fine," "new gasoline" with "Sky Chief Supreme"); the stealth invasion of spoken English by spurious vowels ("nucular," "athaletic"); lunch counters, which he thought resembled pig troughs; television, which he thought should be abolished by constitutional amendment; and dips, about which he wrote, "I must leave to others the rapt pleasure of inserting an oil-exudant potato chip into an unidentifiable viscous mass, enriched by detached pieces of other guests' oil-exudant potato chips, and then extracting and devouring the now highly socialized tidbit." A glass of wine—unless it was a tenth-rate rosé imbibed by a *sans-culotte*—was as far from a dip as it was possible for a foodstuff to be.

Wine was both civilized and civilizing. "Civilization" was the 101st and final word of the subtitle of *The Joys of Wine*, a book my father compiled in 1975 with his friend Sam Aaron, a wine merchant he'd met four decades earlier when both of them were wandering around a Fifty-Seventh Street delicatessen, Diogenes-like, in search of a ripe Brie. *The Joys of Wine*, a Nebuchadnezzar-sized volume stuffed with Picasso etchings and *Punch* cartoons and color photographs of architecturally distinguished châteaux, was so lavish as to be almost pornographic. (Like *Playboy*, it even had gatefolds: maps of vineyards and reproductions of notable labels.) My father wrote in *Joys* that "to take wine into our mouths is to savor a droplet of the river of human history," a pronouncement I found a tad grandiloquent but whose sincerity I did not doubt. He really believed that when he swallowed a great wine, he *incorporated* Western culture: an entire world of history, literature, art, and religion, straight down the esophagus. Just as walking into Chartres Cathedral or standing on Westminster Bridge brought tears to his eyes, so did the thought of what a commanding officer in Napoleon's army told his soldiers, along with an order to present arms, as they passed the vineyard of Clos de Vougeot, a great Burgundy: "My children, it is to protect these beauties that you go to fight."

3

Wager

When I was in the fifth grade, one of the many inappropriate books I took down from the shelves of my parents' seven-thousand-volume library was *Someone Like You*, a collection of very grown-up, very creepy stories by Roald Dahl. There was the one about the man who liked to chop off people's fingers. There was the one about the wife who clubbed her faithless husband to death with a frozen leg of lamb, then roasted the murder weapon and served it to the police detectives for dinner. But my favorite was "Taste," a story about a father, a daughter, and a bottle of wine. ("Taste" was also my father's favorite. He included it in *Dionysus*, a wine-themed anthology he edited that year, and also, later on, in *The Joys of Wine*. I have since learned that Dahl was a wine collector himself who once poured cheap wine into fancy bottles, served them to his unsuspecting guests, listened to them gush, and then revealed that they'd been snookered.)

The father in the story is a stockbroker named Mike

Schofield, an amiable parvenu who, wishing to be a man of culture, has become a collector of books, paintings, and wine. The daughter is a virginal eighteen-year-old named Louise. The scene is a small dinner party at the Schofield residence whose guest of honor is Richard Pratt, a pompous epicure with "a pendulous, permanently open taster's lip, shaped to receive the rim of a glass." Pratt bets his host that he can identify the wine served with the roast beef—a Bordeaux from a vineyard so obscure that Schofield is certain that no one, not even the world's greatest connoisseur, could possibly recognize it.

The stakes are set. If Pratt loses the wager, he will forfeit both his houses. If he wins, Schofield will give him Louise's hand in marriage.

I remember thinking: *Hey, you can't do that!* I also remember asking myself if *my* father would ever make that bet, and confidently answering: *Never.* He would no sooner have treated his daughter so carelessly than he would have written a word product. His parental style was attentive, inventive, and performative. He worked at home, both in Connecticut, where we lived until I was eight, and in Los Angeles, where we moved to be closer to relatives and because my mother imagined, incorrectly, that California would transform my brother Kim and me from nerds with perpetually runny noses into tall, tan, healthy in-crowders who knew how to surf. My father was therefore available around the clock (except in the early morning, since he had the circadian rhythm of an opossum). When he read to us, he equipped the characters with Southern drawls, Scottish burrs, Irish brogues, and

With me and Kim,
circa 1955

French warbles. He entertained us with stories not only about Wally the Wordworm but also about Miniature the Rabbit and his nemesis, Wolfenstein, a wolf whose sneak attacks were repeatedly thwarted by the fact that he had swallowed a Steinway piano, which gave away his location by tinkling. He even let us set up a Ping-Pong table in his study so we could play while he was "working."

Pratt spends an entire page just smelling the claret and taking the first swallow. Then, inch by agonizing inch, he homes in on his target. Saint-Émilion or Graves? Too light. Obviously a Médoc. Margaux? Insufficiently powerful bouquet. Pauillac? Insufficiently pithy flavor. Obviously a Saint-Julien. First or second growth? Neither. Lacks the necessary radiance. Third growth? Perhaps, but more likely a fourth. Château Beychevelle? Getting close. Château Talbot? Too slow to deliver its fruit. By process of elimination: Château Branaire-Ducru. And the year . . . 1934.

"Come on, Daddy," says Louise eagerly, picturing the houses her family is about to win. "Turn it round and let's have a peek."

It is, of course, a Château Branaire-Ducru '34.

At that terrible moment, a uniformed maid brings Pratt—the lout! the cheat! the fiend!—the horn-rimmed spectacles he left in his host's study before dinner, right next to the spot where the wine had been placed to breathe.

When I read the story of this wager, I did not know that whenever my father was invited to dinner by his elder brother, the butler would choose a bottle from the well-stocked cellar and bring it to the table, wrapped in a white linen cloth. The wine would be poured. Each brother would swirl his glass, then sip it, then talk about it, then sip it again, then finally guess the wine. One of them would usually nail it. To the best of my knowledge, Château Branaire-Ducru was never served, no one ever cheated, and the only stake was pride.

It seems improbable that a fifth-grader liked Dahl's nasty little tale of flim-flam and claret. It seems even more improbable that she understood it. But all that talk of Saint-Émilions and Médocs made at least as much sense to me as a conversation about Ramblers and Studebakers would have made to the daughter of a used-car dealer. *We* served claret with *our* roast beef! *We* let it breathe!

I understood that Richard Pratt's wine-snobbery was inseparable from his general ickiness. My father wasn't like him at all. He wasn't like Mike Schofield either. What I didn't understand was that although he bore little resemblance to Schofield the daughter-wagerer, he had more than a little in common with Schofield the parvenu—or feared he did.

4

Ardt

One of my father's touchstones, shoehorned as often as possible into conversations with Kim and me, was a John Galsworthy story called "Quality," about an immigrant shoemaker who fashions boots so beautiful they incarnate the very spirit of footgear. When asked if this is difficult to do, the shoemaker responds, "Id is an Ardt!"

My father was partial to all things fabricated with skill and effort: boots, books, bridges, cathedrals, and, especially, food. He preferred cheese to milk, pâté to liver, braised endive to salad.

There was nothing—not even dips—that he hated more than grapes. If they garnished a serving of, say, Camembert and crackers, he would leave the plate untouched. Kim once asked him, "Daddy, if you love wine so much, why do you hate grapes?"

He replied, "Food should be as far as possible from its origins."

Kim is sure that he was thinking about more than wine.

The "subtext"—a term our father used frequently, since he believed most statements were either too subtle or too disingenuous to be taken at face value—was that he wanted to be as far as possible from his own origins, too. After all, he had put a great deal of skill and effort into fabricating himself. Id vas an Ardt.

In his seventies, he recalled that as a young man he had looked around him and realized that things were run by people who spoke well and who were not Jewish, not poor, and not ugly. He couldn't become a gentile, but there was nothing to stop him from acquiring money and perfect English. The ugliness was a self-deprecatory exaggeration. It is true that *The Wall Street Journal* once referred, not altogether flatteringly, to his "extraordinary physiognomy, a cross between Edward G. Robinson and Charles Laughton"; it is also true that, explaining his fondness for long, thin panatela cigars, preferably Upmann 240s, he once wrote, "As I am, alas, neither long nor thin, my preference for the shape must be compensatory." But his silhouette was streamlined by the expensive clothes he was able to afford in his prime (though he remained a clueless dresser who always needed help choosing them), and, because he was witty, charming, and never, ever vulgar, he rarely had difficulty attracting women.

My father was from Brooklyn, a century before it became fashionable: Brownsville, Canarsie, Bath Beach, Brooklyn Heights, Flatbush, all of them crowded with immigrants and smelling of garbage and noisy with street fights. He described his family as belonging—just barely—

to the lowest level of the lower middle class. He shared a bed with his two brothers in a succession of shabby, triple-locked apartments over a series of unsuccessful drugstores operated by his father, under whose guidance he jerked sodas, prepared salves, rolled pills, sold leeches, and dispensed condoms (which he thought were called "conundrums" and was told were used for storing toothbrushes). His father came from a village near Minsk, his mother from a village in the Ukraine so small it was said you had to enter it sideways. After his birth in 1904, his mother, a nurse, settled on "Clifton" by turning the pages of the Brooklyn telephone directory until she came to a name so fancy she had never heard it before. ("Fancy," he once explained to me, "meant Christian.") "Clifton" didn't last long; it was replaced by the onomatopoetic nickname "Kip" after he suffered an extended bout of the hiccups at the age of one week. His parents owned a samovar and, when he was a boy, taught him how to drink tea with a sugar cube between his teeth. ("It dribbled. Also, I realized it was low class.") He had a large number of female relatives who, whenever he visited, would sidle suffocatingly close and say, "Have a piece of fruit!"—or, as he told Kim and me five decades later, in a mock-Yiddish accent, "Hev a piss *frrrruit*!" He remembered the fruit, and perhaps the relatives, as overripe and unpleasantly squishy. I feel sure this is where the grape phobia came from.

He learned to read at four. He recalled that before he was ten, in the lifelong conflation of reading and eating that would reach its apogee half a century later when he invented Wally the Wordworm, he "devoured" Charles Dickens, Mark Twain, and Thomas Bailey Aldrich along with the Rover Boys, the Pony Rider Boys, the Frank Merriwell series, the Dave Darrin series, more than seventy volumes by Horatio Alger, and an adventure story set in the Belgian Congo that made him an anti-imperialist for the rest of his days. At eight or nine he started writing down what he called his "reactions" to various authors, including Poe and Kipling, in a novel-sized notebook with fake leather covers. At thirteen he read Sophocles, Dante, Milton, and Melville. At fourteen or fifteen he read Maupassant, Meredith, Swinnerton, Chesterton, Gissing, Conrad, Shaw, Yeats, Synge, Wilde, and Wells. He became an expert in ambulatory reading, able to step on and off curbs and avoid bumping into pedestrians while walking to and from the library with a book in front of his face. His family wondered how he would find work when he grew up, since all he seemed able to do was read.

His parents made a point of speaking English at home, rather than Russian or Yiddish, but it was accented and ungrammatical. My father recalled saying to himself, "This is wrong—wrong in the sense that two and two do not equal five, but also practically disadvantageous." With the help of his elder brother, who had been trained in elocution by the drama coach at Boys High in Bedford-Stuyvesant, he learned English "as if it were Latin or Sanskrit," and developed the hyperculti-vated voice—a voice so impeccable no one actually spoke that way except other people from Brooklyn who wished

My father as a senior at Boys High, Class of 1920, already with trademark pompadour

to sound as if they weren't—that would later attract an avalanche of mash notes from female listeners during his years as a radio host and then help to make him, as Wikipedia so felicitously puts it, a prime example of "the highly educated, elegant, patrician raconteurs and pundits regarded by TV executives of that era as appealing to the upper-class owners of expensive early TV sets."

Following class day exercises that featured a Fadiman-devised parody of the ghost scene in *Hamlet*, he graduated from Boys High in January of 1920, when he was fifteen. (Many smart public-school boys of his generation skipped a grade; he skipped two and a half.) Eight months later, he crossed the East River and enrolled at Columbia. When he emerged from the subway at 116th and Broadway, wearing a jacket and a necktie, his first thought was that he'd never seen such a clean street. The round trip from Flatbush took two hours and forty minutes every day.

The journalist Theodore H. White, a rabbi's grandson who commuted in similar fashion from Dorchester to

Harvard (and, before my father arrived on the scene, hoped to marry my mother), divided the Harvard student body of his era into three categories: white men (alumni of New England prep schools); gray men (public-school graduates and students from other parts of the country); and meatballs (local Jewish, Italian, and Irish kids who could not afford to live on campus). When my father arrived at Columbia, he was unquestionably a meatball. He spent his years there refashioning himself, through a strenuous but for the most part enjoyable regimen of self-stuffing, into something approximating *foie gras*.

Two intelligible fields of study lay before him: the Western canon and the WASP social code. He readily mastered the first, progressing with Wally-like avidity through the reading list of John Erskine's General Honors course (Homer, Plato, Aristotle, Virgil, Augustine, Aquinas, Spinoza, Fielding, and Freud, among more than forty others): the wellspring of the Great Books movement. His friend Jacques Barzun considered my father "the bearer of all Western culture since the Greeks" and recalled that every issue of the college literary magazine contained "one or more of his poems—often a sonnet—or an essay, a fragment of philosophy translated from the French, or an imaginary scene between figures in a tragedy by Sophocles." He made substantial headway in the second field of study as well, learning how to comport himself in the living rooms of professors with long Anglo-Saxon pedigrees whose equally pedigreed wives offered him tea from porcelain teapots rather than samovars and smoked salmon on toast points rather than overripe fruit.

The greatest impediment to his social education was the fact that his leisure time—the hallmark of the *beau monde*—was nonexistent. He worked his way through Columbia, not only paying the bulk of his own tuition ($256 a year, of which a state scholarship covered less than half) but saving enough for an occasional stretch in a dormitory ($67.50 a semester). He washed dishes, waited tables, sorted mail, tutored classmates, took attendance, sold magazine subscriptions, ran a bookshop in Penn Station, wrote reviews for *The Nation*, listened to a retired Wall Street speculator with a weak bladder declaim Shakespeare's erotic verse, gave lessons on French symbolist poetry to a blind actress, served as a companion to a mentally impaired boy who enjoyed tossing him down a small hill in Harlem, and broke in pipes.

Broke in pipes?

I remember him patiently explaining this to me when I was a child. The rich boys smoked expensive pipes; new pipes were unpleasant to smoke until a layer of carbon had built up inside the bowl; he was therefore paid to pre-smoke them for a few weeks. This struck me as a Sisyphean tragedy. (He had, of course, recounted to Kim and me the myth of Sisyphus, along with the other essential chestnuts of Greek mythology.) What could be worse than having to give up something just when it got good and start all over again with something bad?

The rich boys were the ones who bought the upper-crust regalia advertised in the *Columbia Daily Spectator*: solid gold Sheaffer pencils, Rogers Peet luggage, Tom Logan golf shoes, Earl & Wilson detachable collars ("The informal dance at the country club is not so informal that you can afford to wear a collar you are not sure of"). My father should have hated them, but when he talked about the rich boys his tone was always amused and more than a little envious. He didn't want to dethrone them; he wanted to become them.

I now see my father's envy as a painful but potent motivator. His generation of self-invented men—most of them Jews, the sons of grocers, peddlers, druggists, tailors, haberdashers, fishmongers, pants pressers, night watchmen, suspender makers, jewelry salesmen—fell into two categories. When they left their immigrant neighborhoods for college, they took a good look at the WASP establishment and were either so angry that they wanted to tear it down or so dazzled that they couldn't wait to join the club. In my father's Columbia cohort, which over the years has become legendary for its abundance of public intellectuals, the demolishers became Communists and fellow travelers: Herbert Solow, David Zablodowsky, grad student Felix Morrow, and Whittaker Chambers, one of the few gentiles in the group, though not a wealthy one. (It was my father who, perhaps inadvisedly, encouraged Chambers, until that point an admirer of Calvin Coolidge, to read *The Communist Manifesto*. Chambers later became a Soviet spy before switching sides and becoming a vehemently anti-Communist journalist.) Chambers called the circle *ernste Menschen*—serious men—whose ardor for learning he attributed to "a struggle with a warping poverty impossible for those who have not glimpsed it to imagine." Most of the joiners became academics: Mortimer Adler, Meyer Schapiro, and Lionel Trilling, a middle-class boy with a narrower river to cross but an equally powerful thirst for Western culture. I don't think anyone wanted to join more fervently than my father. Though he flirted with left-wing politics, it was hard to declare lifelong solidarity with the working class when he was trying so hard to stay out of it.

You might assume that wine appreciation was among his newly acquired social graces. Not yet. It was Prohibition. My father frequented speakeasies in the West Forties, Fifties, and Sixties. Who would go to the trouble of whispering a password through a peephole and giving a secret handshake while worrying about the possibility of a police raid, and then say, "May I please have a glass of Gevrey-Chambertin Clos Saint-Jacques?"—which, in any event, would almost certainly have been unavailable because hard liquor was so much more profitable to bootleg than wine? During Prohibition, whiskey and gin became far more popular than wine and beer because they packed more alcohol per ounce and were thus comparatively cheaper to transport and easier to hide. Customers came not to sip a leisurely glass with dinner but to get soused. (Or jazzed, jingled, piffed, piped, owled, oiled, canned, zozzled, squiffy, sloppy, scrooched, spifflicated, loaded to the muzzle, fried to the hat, slopped to the ears, stewed to the gills, and lit up like the Commonwealth, to mention some of the 105 terms for drunkenness that Edmund Wilson, who would succeed my father as book critic for *The New Yorker*, compiled during the twenties.)

My father introduced Lionel and Diana Trilling to each other in a speakeasy. As an old woman, Diana told him, "I don't think that I had a date, whether it was with you or Lionel or anybody we knew in common, in which I didn't come home drunk." The Trillings favored Bullfrogs and Brandy Alexanders. My father favored pousse-cafés: seven layers of liqueurs (grenadine, crème de cacao, maraschino, curaçao, crème de menthe, parfait d'amour, and cognac, poured in sequence, heaviest first), whose colors he could never quite make out because of the limitations of speakeasy illumination. Nonetheless, he recalled, "I had full confidence that, together with the reciting of Swinburne, they made up the iridescent symbol of abandonment."

He graduated from Columbia in 1925 with a Phi Beta Kappa key paid for by one of his professors, since he couldn't afford the fifteen dollars; a reputation as a wit so celebrated that fellow students crowded into elevators with him, hoping to catch a Fadimanism or two between floors; the ability to mingle with people who did not drink tea with sugar cubes between their teeth; and unsullied oenological virginity. Until he filled that last gap, his education would not be complete. Reading about Western civilization wasn't the same thing as swallowing it.

5

Gods

I was sent to private schools chosen to scrub away any vestiges of meatballdom. If I had any, they would have come solely from the paternal side. My mother was descended from distinguished Utah Mormons, an extraction so far removed from the Jewish/WASP and Brooklyn/Manhattan dichotomies that she was free to move with equal, insouciant ease between the world my father had left behind and the one to which he had immigrated.

When I was in the sixth grade at one of those private schools, I was assigned two long themes.

In the first assignment, we were to write about a Greek god. Which one do you think I chose? Correct. In "Drink to Dionysus," after describing how the fun-loving god with the crown of grape leaves learned to make wine and "journeyed through Greece and far-off lands, giving wine to human beings," I observed that Apollo, who had for no apparent reason barged onto the last page of my theme,

> was kind, sensible, and rational. This is the "correct" personality for a civilized person to have, but that few possess. So many people are like Dionysus, though, the god who symbolized the crazy, uncontrolled, irrational, but enjoyable way of life.

What must my teacher, Mrs. Louise Smith, have thought of this peculiar assertion? Did she have any inkling that I had somehow recognized I was more Apollonian than Dionysian—doomed to a life of carefully controlled cerebration, good at being correct, bad at letting go?

In the second assignment, we were to write a report on a foreign country, presented "creatively" in the form of an ersatz diary. Mine (seventeen pages, because I was such an Apollonian goody-goody) was titled "La Belle France." Along with the population of Marseille and the number of people who had committed suicide by jumping off the Eiffel Tower, it contained the valuable intelligence that "Bordeaux is bottled in abruptly-shouldered bottles, while Burgundy bottles have more sloping shoulders." (Duh. I'd known that since I was six.) After "visiting" Bordeaux, I wrote:

> I cannot describe the endless underground cellars, where the wine is aged in casks for a year or so before bottling. The coolness, and the odor of aging wine is unique. We tasted the wine. I thought it would be strong and

sour (a word shunned by wine connoisseurs—they call it dry). But it was lovely, not at all like the wine my father has at home.

The last sentence was a joke, though it may have sailed right over Mrs. Smith's head. I knew that the hundreds of bottles my father kept on X-shaped racks in the pantry of our house in Los Angeles—laid horizontally, he explained, so their corks would not dry out—contained lovely wine, even if my palate was not yet ready to appreciate it. (When we'd lived in Connecticut, the bottles he planned to drink during the next few weeks had been stored in his office and the rest in the basement, near the bench where my brother performed chemistry experiments, many of which involved small explosions. Kim always worried that he'd blow up the wine and our father would never speak to him again.)

The final diary entry in "La Belle France" was ostensibly written in Paris. On my last night, "as I looked up at the stars, pinpoints against a black velvet pincushion, I realized how much I would miss France. I had grown to be a part of it." I'm not sure about the pincushion, but I know where "I had grown to be a part of it" came from. As my father had told me many times, that was how *he* felt about France.

6

Kismet

My father went to Paris for the first time in 1927. He was twenty-three. "My wife had by a few weeks preceded me there," he wrote in "Brief History of a Love Affair," "so that when I arrived she was already wearing the city like a glove." That summary left out one or two minor details, including the fact that the wife in question had preceded him because she had run off with an Italian count. (Or a baron. My father told the story both ways. Once, when I tried to pin him down, he answered, with a wicked grin, "I can't remember. Which is better?")

In most households, a story about a beautiful but unfaithful first wife might not be ideal dinner-table fodder, but in our home the Retrieval of Polly was a family favorite—enjoyed even by my mother, the second wife—partly because my father's narration lent it an irresistibly epic quality, like the quest for the Golden Fleece or the Holy Grail, and partly because we all knew the real prize was not Polly. It was the glass of white Graves he drank in the lunchroom of the Bon Marché department store.

But I'm getting ahead of myself.

The initial hurdle was financing the quest. One of his Columbia professors introduced him to Bennett Cerf, the chairman of Random House; he asked Cerf if there was any available work; Cerf asked him if he knew German; and presto! He had an assignment to translate two volumes of Nietszche for the Modern Library. Depending on the rendition, he was paid either a hundred dollars apiece or a hundred dollars for the pair. Either way, it was enough for a third-class passage to Le Havre. Because his shared cabin had no table, he spent all day in the ship's bar, a glass of warm beer (he still had never tasted wine!) next to his German-English dictionary as he translated *Ecce Homo* and *The Birth of Tragedy*, the latter of which is still in print, nine decades later, in a Dover Thrift Edition.

The second hurdle was winning back Polly's affections. My father provided few details about this phase at the dinner table, though he told me, many years later, that he and Polly had stayed in "a lovely little room in a fifth-rate hotel," the Hôtel Rue de l'Abbé Grégoire on the Left Bank. "We had a great time," he said. "We were young and healthy. There was nothing else to do but eat and practice our French and screw. It was a very balanced life."

One of the first milestones in this balanced life was lunch at the aforementioned department store. In "Brief History of a Love Affair," he recalls that it was a brilliant August day, "a day like a pearl."

With our lunch my wife, already to me formidably learned in these matters, ordered a cheap white Graves. Its deep straw color was pleasing to the eye. Even in this busy department store it was served with just a graceful allusion to a flourish. It was properly chilled against the midsummer heat. For the first time I tasted *wine*. It must have sent me into mild catatonia for it was not until perhaps sixty seconds later that I seemed to hear my wife's voice say from far away, "You have the most peculiar, *foolish* smile on your face." "Do I?" was all I could reply.

He always said this first taste felt less like a new experience than like an old one that had been waiting all his life for him to catch up to it. He tried to describe it by analogy—it was like Plato's doctrine of reminiscence, or like the moment when the hero of Conrad's "Youth" reaches the East, or like Napoleon's realization that he was born to be a soldier—but invariably fell back on the language of eros. The Graves spoke to him: "I am your fate. You are mine. Love me."

I've often wondered what would have happened if Prohibition hadn't coincided with my father's college years. Would he have tried wine at a forgettable party in Morningside Heights instead of in Paris, during one of the happiest moments of his life? In that case, would the connection have felt less compelling? Or what if Polly had ordered a couple of Rémy Martins instead of that bottle of Graves? Might he have fallen in love with cognac? I don't know the answer, but I know what *he* would have said: Paris helped, young love helped, the perfection of that August afternoon helped, but he and wine were made for each other. Kismet.

The Retrieval of Polly had some ancillary sub-tales: the time he ordered *fraises des bois* and, failing to understand that the accompanying tureen of *crème Chantilly* was intended for all the establishment's patrons, ate it all himself; the time he realized he couldn't afford the restaurant he and Polly had just walked into, and attempted to save their pride and their pocketbooks with a budget-friendly order of melon—but mispronounced it, and was alarmed to see the waiter emerge from the kitchen bearing a platter on which reposed an enormous fish: a *merlan*. When he told these stories, he wanted us to laugh at what a rube he'd been, but also to understand that each embarrassment, like each of the dozens of bottles of wine on which he was proud to overspend during those six charmed weeks, was a lesson in civilization.

7

Homesick

When I went to Paris the summer before my sixteenth birthday, I was, of course, no wine virgin. What Fadiman over the age of ten could have been? But the watered-down glasses of my childhood didn't count. I was practically grown up. It was time to have my own Platonic-Conradian-Napoleonic-Fadimanian moment. I was ready to love wine.

There was plenty of it, from the glass of generic red I was served on Air France (things were different in 1969), to the omnipresent *vins de pays* on the table of my host family, to the Mascara Noir (can this really have been the name of a wine, or was it a *melon/merlan*-esque misunderstanding?) that I shared with some boys before an evening at the Comédie-Française, to the bottles lugged by a throng of fellow students on a raucous promenade down the Champs-Élysées on which an earnest young guitarist's attempts to sing "Where Have All the Flowers Gone?" were drowned out by shouts of "Pass the

Bordeaux!" Opportunity abounded. There were only two problems. The first was that I was miserable. I eventually fell in with a copacetic circle of intellectuals who quoted Sartre and smoked Gauloises (I did the former, so they forgave me for not doing the latter), but at the start I was a homesick, jet-lagged, self-conscious nerd from L.A. on an Eastern prep-school summer program who felt more or less the way her father must have felt when he crossed the river from Brooklyn to Manhattan. In other words, for the first time in my life, I was a meatball.

The second problem was that, as I put it, "I try to drink wine whenever I can, but I still don't especially like it."

I know that's what I said because my father saved the nine letters I sent home that summer, all addressed to "The Clifton Fadimans," as if my mother were an invisible subset. (I found them in his files after he died.) I saved my mother's three letters—models of solicitude on the importance of sufficient sleep and a good breakfast—and the fifteen I received from my father, addressed to "Mlle. Anne Fadiman." Between "Dearest Anne" and "All my love, Daddy," he managed to stuff in so much reassuring advice—disregard the opinions of mediocre people, remember that discomfort is fodder for future writing, take more walks, speak more French, don't take things so seriously, to hell with marks ("and Engels too")—that he made me feel not like an outcast among cool preppies but like a Trockenbeerenauslese among *vins ordinaires*.

When I was in middle school, I had considered my

father an assiduous parent but too smart, too square, too odd, and too old. (He was forty-nine when I was born, sixty when I started seventh grade, sixty-five when I went to France.) My friends' fathers were very different. They radiated West Coast informality; he preferred not just East Coast decorum but what he called "English good manners," by which he meant manners that were unostentatious, none too chummy, and, in their ideal form, practiced by someone who could trace his ancestry to the Norman Conquest (not before, since decent wine had arrived with the French) and owned a small Palladian country house in Hertfordshire. My friends' fathers were tan and sportive; my father's résumé listed his hobbies as wine and "the avoidance of exercise." Whenever my school's annual Father-Daughter Picnic rolled around, I left him at home and tagged along with my cousin, whose father was younger, taller, more likely to acquit himself creditably in a volleyball game, and generally less embarrassing. My father never said a word about being ditched. Only years later, after I became a parent myself, did I realize how much I must have hurt him.

But I was fifteen now, just beginning to move out of the peak season of anti-parental eye-rolling, and in France I didn't have to worry what anyone would think of him, since he was more than five thousand miles away. I was surprised how glad I was to hear that he missed me "dreadfully" and watched the mail "like a hawk" in hopes of an aerogramme with a French postmark. I appreciated his promise that he would drink a toast to me on Bastille Day. Even when I was feeling down, I shared his tender feelings for Paris. In fact, I had to admit I had more in common with him than with most of the students on my trip, whose idea of a good time was "going to a discothèque, meeting other people from the group, getting drunk, getting sick." He dismissed these activities with a single, satisfying word: "vacuous."

But there was one vital thing we did not yet have in common. "Keep on trying the wine," he wrote. "*Suddenly it will seem right and habitual.*" (How many fathers today would offer that counsel to their fifteen-year-old daughters?) On a side trip to the château country, a glass of Vouvray—which I dutifully described as "a white pétillant demi-sec"—went down with reasonable success ("I'm improving, Daddy"), but that was only because it was cold and I was hot. I would have preferred Coca-Cola.

When our group traveled through southern France, I wrote my parents: "Trumpets! I fully expect you to faint or do something equally dramatic when I tell you that M. Cosnard took me to La Pyramide day before yesterday." I then listed everything I had eaten. My father had told me numerous times that La Pyramide, a triple-*étoile* establishment in Vienne, was the best restaurant in the world. He responded, "God, what a meal! One of my great ambitions has been to eat there. I never will—but to think of my little girl guzzling away at ten courses plus champagne is compensatory."

Actually, it wasn't champagne. It was Brut Crémant '62, a sparkling white wine with a slightly less ebullient fizz than champagne. (If it's not made in Champagne, it can't be called champagne, but as far as I was concerned, this was close enough.) Under the benevolent gaze of Monsieur Jean Pierre Cosnard des Closets, the director of our program, I progressed through our ten courses at a table laid with beautiful napery and more forks than I had ever seen in my life, and consumed, in small but inexorable increments, at least half the contents of a bottle that seemed to grow larger with every sip. I never told my father that my newfound capacity for alcohol had sprung not from incipient oenophilia but from fear for my safety. The more I drank, the less there was for Monsieur Cosnard: a prudent strategy, I thought, given that we would soon get into his Mercedes and that he liked to drive eighty-five miles an hour in the two-way passing lane. By the fifth glass, I felt as if I'd taken one too many whirls on a rickety ride at a down-at-the-heel amusement park.

On the way to Avignon, Monsieur Cosnard asked me to help find the route. I might have done a better job had I held the map right side up.

8

Multihyphenate

My father kept in his files a black-and-white photograph of a portrait painted long before I was born. He sits at a large desk, one hand curled under his chin in *Penseur* fashion, the other holding an elegant fountain pen, an artfully fanned stack of blank pages ready to receive the words that are about to flow from it. He wears a velvet smoking jacket with a shawl collar and a Byronic white shirt open one button too many. His dark blond hair—always his best feature—billows above his high forehead in a pompadour whose marine undulations, innocent of Vitalis, seem held in place by the sheer power of the brain waves that emanate from below. He looks like a man who'll be damned if he'll be cuckolded by either a count or a baron but is working a little too hard to prevent it.

He also looks like a man who owns a walking stick (he does), smokes expensive pipes he is permitted to enjoy past the break-in period (he does), and has started to lay down a wine cellar (he has).

When my father returned from Paris to New York, he could tell a Burgundy from a Bordeaux without looking at the shape of the bottle, and knew that although he loved the former, he loved the latter even more. I always suspected this was because Bordeaux are named after châteaux. *Castles.* The antithesis of an apartment over a Brooklyn drugstore.

He had to wait six years before he could legally drink either one. Prohibition was repealed in 1933; the American wine industry began to reinvent itself; he no longer had to whisper passwords through speakeasy peepholes, which was a good thing, since he had graduated from pousse-cafés. What a heady time it must have been! For fourteen years, the only wine that had passed most American lips was home-brewed from grape juice, grapes crushed in bathtubs, or "grape bricks," concentrated blocks that came with painstakingly disingenuous instructions: "Do not place this brick in a one gallon crock, add sugar and water, cover, and let stand for seven days or else an illegal alcoholic beverage will result." Now hundreds of California wineries (of little interest to my father) were springing up, and dozens of merchants were scrambling to start wine-importing firms (of greater interest). One of these merchants was Frank Schoonmaker, a Princeton dropout who had decided that the best way to turn ignoramuses into customers was to become a wine writer. Schoonmaker became a friend of my father's and began to teach him about wine. By 1935, two years after Repeal, my father felt ready to start collecting.

"Brief History of a Love Affair" included a description

of his Cellar Book. He capitalized it; so shall I. A Cellar Book is a record of wines, vintages, dealers, costs, and dates of acquisition, accompanied by tasting notes. After making use of the earliest one, published in 1766, one wine lover wrote that a Cellar Book should be "as necessary an appendage to every gentleman's writing-desk or escritoire as his pocket-book to his pocket." My father wrote that the date of his own earliest entry was "October 17, 1935, at which time I seem to have laid down a dozen Morey, Clos des Lambrays '29 at a price ($28) that today induces wistful dreams. 'Quite beautiful' is the notation under 'Remarks.'"

This is how he ended the essay:

I turn the pages of my Cellar Book. Two lines, appearing toward the end of *The Waste Land*, slip unbidden into my mind:

> *London Bridge is falling down falling down falling down . . .*
>
> *These fragments I have shored against my ruins . . .*

When I first read those lines as a child, I had no idea why my father had quoted them, but I knew they were dark. Now I understand that the bottles laid down by the man in the velvet smoking jacket were both a reminder of all he had achieved since leaving Brooklyn and a bulwark against the future. He would get old. His pompadour would turn white. His body would fail. But he would still have these magnificent wines, and they would improve with each passing decade.

Clos des Lambrays was a *Premier Cru* Burgundy (since elevated to *Grand Cru*). Need I mention that 1929 was a Great Year—even though, since only six years had passed, it was not yet fully dusted with the hoar of legend? Twelve bottles of Clos des Lambrays from a comparable year in our own century—say, 2005, the best in recent memory—currently cost about $2,600. In other words, now only the inordinately rich can buy fine wine, whereas in 1935 my father could. Still, $28 was a lot of money (the equivalent of nearly $500 today), and the Clos des Lambrays wasn't the only case he laid down. How did he afford it?

He had confounded the expectations of both his family, who had thought he was good for nothing but reading books all day (who could possibly make a living from *that*?), and his high school classmates. He once told me with a half smile that, perhaps for similar reasons, they had voted him Least Likely to Succeed. Also Politest.

At twenty-eight, he was still reading books all day, but as the editor-in-chief of Simon & Schuster. He got his first job there by bringing a folder of one hundred neatly typed book ideas—"not 99 or 101"—to a dinner meeting with Max Schuster. Schuster said, "What makes you think you would be helpful to us?" My father presented his folder and said, "This is it, sir." One of those hundred ideas, the publication of the *Ripley's Believe It or Not!* cartoons from the *New York Evening Post* in book form, made Simon & Schuster a small fortune. Soon after his arrival, he commissioned his college friend Whittaker Chambers to translate *Bambi* from the German (the text was safely apolitical) and, in the first of many instances in which his literary crushes stepped off the page into his own life, invited John Galsworthy ("Id is an Ardt") to write the introduction. This too was a bestseller. He also published *The Complete Wine Book*, by his friend Frank Schoonmaker and the *Herald Tribune* columnist Tom Marvel, which helped tens of thousands of readers graduate from grape bricks to French Burgundies and, according to Ford Madox Ford, left an "admirable aftertaste."

At twenty-nine, he was the book critic of *The New Yorker*. (He preferred to call himself a "reviewer," observing that "my colleagues and myself are often called critics, a consequence of the amiable national trait that turns Kentuckians into colonels and the corner druggist into Doc.") He praised Sinclair Lewis and Christina Stead but called Gertrude Stein a "master in the art of making nothing happen very slowly" and William Faulkner "our greatest literary sadist," an author whose readers deserved, on making it through one of his novels alive, to be met by a brandy-bearing St. Bernard.

At thirty-four, he was the emcee of *Information Please*. I heard so many stories around the dinner table about his NBC radio quiz show that its title had a primordial ring, and I was middle-aged before I realized that it came from *somewhere else*—the request every American in the thirties had made thousands of times to that now-mythic figure, the telephone operator—instead of being the riverhead from which all other iterations had flowed. At its peak, fifteen million people, including Justice Felix Frankfurter and a New York cab driver who

The Information Please *regulars: Oscar Levant, John Kieran, the Grand Inquisitor, and Franklin P. Adams, circa 1940*

tried to avoid fares between 8:30 and 9:00 every Tuesday night, listened to my father preside over a panel of wits who, as *Time* put it, were "baited, stung, encouraged, wounded" by a series of pointed questions. He was called not only Matador Fadiman but the Toscanini of Quiz, the Grand Inquisitor, and a captain who could play any position, though he once told me he thought of himself as more of a lion tamer. Each week sixty thousand listeners sent in questions. If they stumped the experts, they were awarded prize money (to the *thrrring-thrrring* of a cash register) and, starting in the second year, a set of the *Encyclopædia Britannica*. The right answer wasn't important; what mattered was the pun, the ad lib, the deliciously acidulous riposte. My father considered the quiz format merely an armature around which to build a conversation, one that was friendly but deliberately formal. He and the panelists—columnist Franklin P. Adams, sportswriter John Kieran, and pianist Oscar Levant—always called each other Mister. The guests who joined the panel each week included Mister Hitchcock, Mister Willkie, Mister Woollcott, Mister Karloff, Mister Durante, and two Mister Marxes. Harpo, of course, had to stay in character and therefore said not a word. If he knew an answer, he whistled a snatch from an appropriate popular song; if he didn't, he repeatedly honked a small horn to drown out the competition. My father asked his panelists to recite the first stanza of "Paul Revere's Ride"; specify the number of toes they would see in the footprint of a chicken; explain why it was necessary for the Byrd Antarctic Expedition to carry a refrigerator; and distinguish between dodo, zobo, koto, yo-yo, Popo, bolo, and locofoco. On one show, he intoned plummily, "The next question, gentlemen and Mrs. Barrymore"—Ethel was a guest—*"demands your closest attention. It cannot be repeated. It comes from Mr. Mort Weisinger, of Great Neck, New York, and is divided into two parts. The first part: What is the name of the author of this question? The second part: Where does he live?"* The panel was stumped. On another show, he asked the men in his audience to close their eyes and try to remember the color of their ties. A listener who was driving with his radio on obediently followed these instructions, crashed into a telephone pole, lost a fender, and sued the show's sponsor. My father was delighted by the reach of his influence.

He spent a decade at each of these jobs. It was only when I looked up the dates that I realized there were at least a dozen years when he held two at once. But that was just the tip of the vocational iceberg. He claimed that during this stretch he never had fewer than seven jobs and at one point had thirteen. He was once referred to as a "celebrated multihyphenate." The multiplicity of hyphens hadn't changed much since he worked his way through Columbia, the only difference being that instead of a dishwasher-waiter-pipesmoker-etc.-etc.-etc., he was now an editor-critic-emcee-teacher-translator-lecturer-columnist-essayist-anthologist-agent-consultant. The "consultant" was to Samuel Goldwyn, who hired him to recommend books that would make good movies, ignored his recommendations, and, for reasons my father never figured out, labored under the unshakable conviction that his name was Mr. Goodleman. Interviewers never failed to remark on my father's industry, sometimes with awe and sometimes with distaste, as for the grind who studies all night and ruins the curve. One called his *modus operandi* "mass production." He worked as many as eighteen hours a day, seven days a week, holidays included. He was constantly, pathologically, insanely busy.

That's how he afforded the wine.

9

Initiation

I teach undergraduates. Many of them get drunk three nights a week. (Few classes meet on Friday now, so weekends start on Thursday afternoon.) For the heavier drinkers, many of them women, many of them underage, the pattern has become standardized: four to eight shots consumed with friends, before heading out to a party, just in case the alcohol runs out by the time they reach the main event (one of my students likens this to squirrels loading up on nuts before the winter); at the party, huge handles of cheap vodka, all with Russian-sounding names although they are produced in the United States; Coke, Pepsi, and orange juice to render the vodka swallowable; if it's a frat, grain-alcohol punch; red Solo cups; loud music; dancing; darkness; sex, sometimes consensual, sometimes not, sometimes too blurred to remember.

By contrast, my own college days were as poignantly, irrecoverably innocent as the time my father asked the *Information Please* panelists to recite their Social Security numbers to millions of listeners. (None of them could.) When I was a student at Harvard, "to party" was not yet an infinitive. I was vaguely aware that football players drank beer and boys in Final Clubs drank cocktails. Knowing how to mix martinis seemed a weirdly grown-up skill, like knowing how to tie the bow ties I saw dangling from the club boys' wing collars as they wove down Mount Auburn Street late at night with well-dressed girls on their arms.

But the people I hung out with were either serious intellectuals who were too busy thinking empyrean thoughts to drink much of anything or serious outdoorsmen—members of the Outing Club, my chief extracurricular activity—who drank hot cocoa in their mountain tents. Perhaps because it was not part of my normal routine, or perhaps because I was reading so much poetry by inebriated English Romantics, intoxication seemed like something I should learn about. A necessary milestone. An initiation.

I had, of course, gotten drunk when I was fifteen, while lunching with Monsieur Cosnard des Closets. But the Brut Crémant hadn't been on my own terms. I hadn't *elected* to get drunk; my intemperance was prompted by my desire neither to die on Autoroute A7 nor to be rude. (I might not have received the prize for Politest, but both my parents had taught me manners.) So one weekend in the winter of 1972, during my sophomore year, I drove to a farmhouse in southern New Hampshire with my friend Peter for the express purpose of getting spifflicated under conditions that were pleasant, voluntary, and safe. There was no question what we would drink. Peter had grown up in Europe, so he was hardly a stranger to wine. And even though I seldom drank it, wine still figured large in my personal mythology. "You talked about it all the time," Peter told me recently. "I remember you mentioning Château d'Yquem more than once. You had a sort of reverence. It was like reciting the names of the saints." When I heard that, a little whoosh of memory rolled in: how it had felt to leave my family for a world in which no one knew or cared about those holy mysteries, and, like a Catholic among heathens, to struggle to protect their sacredness. My insistence may have come partly from my uncertainty about the strength of my own faith.

Peter and I were eighteen. In those days, there was nothing out of the ordinary about spending a weekend alone with a boy with whom you were not sleeping, though I knew Peter wished our platonic relationship were otherwise. The previous year, he had sent me a love letter—the best one I have ever received—in which he wrote, "Every part of me loves every part of you." He would, in fact, have made an excellent boyfriend, but I can see that only now, more than forty years later. We are still friends. I was Best Human at his wedding. He was a bridesperson at mine.

I've asked Peter if he remembers what kind of wine we drank in New Hampshire. He doesn't. We agree that it was a French or Italian red, either two bottles or a magnum. He had borrowed both the car and the farmhouse from a generous family for whom he had worked as an au pair, so perhaps the wine was borrowed too, in which case it was better than anything we could have afforded ourselves. He does remember that he was on edge that weekend because in a few days he would find out his Vietnam draft lottery number, and his Conscientious Objector statement, along with several college papers, was overdue.

We cooked beef stew together. We poured some of the wine into it and drank the rest. After a while, the room spun and my sentences went on way too long. My Apollonian desire for control cut in. I put down my glass.

Peter kept on drinking. He wept. There were confessions of frustration. Longing. Loneliness. Heartbreak. It hadn't turned out to be so safe here after all.

I followed him into the bathroom. He knelt in front of the toilet. I still remember his heaving shoulders. The smell of his vomit. My hands on his head. The snowy darkness outside the window.

10

Counterfeit

By any measure, my father had made it. But he didn't believe it. Even though he possessed an encyclopedic knowledge of Western literature (which, in that time and place, was viewed as the only kind there was); even though his linguistic facility was so fabled that John Kieran had said, "Be careful to specify when ordering whether you want English, French, German, or medieval Latin"; even though *Time* had called him the smartest book reviewer in the country; even though Dorothy Thompson had included him on her list of ideal party guests, on a par with Noël Coward and ahead of all past, present, and future presidents; even though Charlie Chaplin had called him "gifted and cultured" and E. B. White had called him "simply swell"; even though, from his forties to his eighties, he topped off his writer-editor-lecturer income with lucrative stints as a television host and commentator, all the while cheerfully biting the hand that fed him by casting witty aspersions on the idiot box;

My father the cigarette peddler, during one of his television emcee gigs, 1952

even though, as he put it to me, the maîtres d'hôtel of Manhattan recognized him "and all that horseshit"; even though, in the depths of the Depression, he could afford a velvet smoking jacket and a wine cellar—nonetheless, both at the peak of his fame and for the rest of his life, he considered himself an outsider.

This was no secret, at least not within the family. We all knew he felt like a man who has been admitted by mistake to a gentlemen's club and, as soon as he is discovered, will be booted out the service entrance. He once wrote that he would never have "the ease, the charm, the grace of movement of those who have been sure of themselves from the cradle." Whenever he started sounding that note, I could scarcely prevent myself from shouting, "What a load of bullshit!" (Or, rather, horseshit, his preferred obscenity, since he had probably never been to a farm and had read about bulls only in Hemingway, whereas horses figured prominently in English novels.) He was the most cultivated man I knew. And the two most cultivated things about him—books and wine— weren't some fancy facade; they were *him*. How could he not see that?

In his old age, he showed me a letter he had written years earlier to Dorothy Van Doren (the widow of Mark Van Doren, his favorite Columbia professor), with whom he'd conducted what he called "an Adams-Jefferson correspondence" that lasted for decades. The letter described his plans for a book-length essay addressed to his children, to be read after his death. "I am quite convinced," he wrote, "that our whole culture makes it difficult, if not impossible, for children ever really to know their parents."

The book was to be called *Outside, Looking In*. He explained:

Its basic *drang* would turn on my so-called "career." In every case my tiny successes have always seemed to occur in a vacuum because at no time could I feel that I was experiencing them within a culture of which I was a part. The nearest analogy is a performed play: the actor knows that though he engages in heroic activities, he is not a real hero but only a technician, in this case solving a problem in impersonation.

> . . . I remember, when I got my job on the *New
> Yorker*, or won notoriety as a radio hack, or achieved
> anything else usually called success, my immediate reac-
> tion was: "This is a fraud, a charade, and I am either a
> counterfeiter or an actor."

He eventually gave up on the idea of writing the book
and decided I might as well read the letter while he was
still alive. I remember his face the night he showed it to
me. His mouth was curled in an odd way. His expression contained both resignation and something akin to
disgust.

That night, he told me that although he felt grateful
to the country in which he had spent his entire life, he
had never felt truly a part of it. He contrasted himself
with Jacques Barzun, who felt completely at home in the
United States even though he had not arrived from
Europe until he was thirteen. (Jacques, a well-known cultural historian, had been my father's only Columbia friend
from an upper-crust family. He was French and gentile,
raised among avant-garde intellectuals in a bucolic village
outside Paris and then in the posh 16th Arrondissement;
as a child, he had been dandled on Apollinaire's knee in
the salon his parents hosted every Saturday afternoon.
Even after fifty years of friendship, my father did not
consider himself Jacques's social equal.)

My father had given a lot of thought to his sense of
inferiority and concluded that its source was his brother
Ed, his elder by five years. He had looked up to Ed even
more than he had looked down on his parents. Ed was

the president of the Boys High student council, the president of the literary society, the vice president of the Correct English Club, the editor of the school magazine, the winner of the gold medal in the declamation contest, the star of all the plays, the class valedictorian, and 6'1". (My father was 5'8½". He never omitted the ½; he wanted credit for every micron.) Everything Ed did, my father did. When he was five, Ed taught him all forty-six of the state capitals and brought him to school to show him off. Ed was the first to cross the East River to Columbia; he made my father, then thirteen, read the entirety of his own English literature textbook and assigned him essays on Hakluyt and Spenser. Ed was the first to cross the Atlantic to Paris; he returned with a perfect French accent, whereas my father's was merely very good. Although Ed became a wealthy businessman whose ventures in radio, television, and real estate paid for the fine French bottles that provisioned their wine-guessing contests (not to mention the butler who served them), my father became more famous. But even when more than a tenth of the population of the United States was listening to him every Tuesday night, he could never be *taller* than Ed. Or, for that matter, than his younger brother, Bill (5'10"), a successful Hollywood producer who also laid down a respectable wine cellar. When my father was an old man, there were occasional moments of distraction in which the names of his sons and his younger brother were more or less interchangeable, but he never, ever called any of them Ed, who constituted a category of one.

He considered his insecurity one of the factors that

had contributed to his success (or, as he would have put it, his "so-called success"). It had, for instance, elicited the bulging folder he had handed to Max Schuster in 1927. "What produced the hundred ideas?" he once asked me rhetorically. "Not intelligence, not ingenuity, not knowledge. Fear. The fear that I couldn't sell myself the way a real, proper young man six feet tall could have, who looked as if he had more than one suit, could speak well, came from the right background, and could talk about friends who might be useful in the publishing business." I thought he was done, but he paused and then said, "I had none of these things. I was a little stinker."

Those were his exact words. I know because when I was thirty, my boss at *Life* magazine thought it might be nice if I wrote a puff-ish piece about my father on the occasion of his eightieth birthday. It occurred to me that as part of my "research," I could tape hours and hours of conversation, most of it on topics I knew I would never mention in my story, and get *Life* to pay for the transcription. I hoped that if I ever had children, they might want to listen to the tapes someday. Needless to say, the "little stinker" comment did not make it into the pages of *Life*. I still have the tapes, thirty-three-year-old cassettes I am afraid to digitize lest they get broken in the process. (I know that's faulty logic.) I told my father the conversations were "an excuse to find out what is going on in your mind." He replied, "I feel very flattered that you should give a damn."

One of the things we talked about was the Train Dream. He'd had the same recurring dream for decades, even after we moved to California and he traveled only by car or airplane. Its plot was simple: He failed to make a train. One morning, while he was on a trip to New York with my mother, he told her he'd had the dream the previous night. "You missed that train *again*?" she said, as if it had come thundering through the Hotel Intercontinental. He told me that the atmosphere of the Train Dream could be characterized by a single monosyllable: loss.

I am sure that is true. But I don't think he kept missing the train because of what he had lost. I think he kept missing it because he never fully trusted what he had gained.

Sometimes his self-deprecation was an act. It was part of English good manners. A conversation with him could be like a badminton game in which you were supposed to swat a compliment in his direction and he was supposed to swat back a bit of hyperbolic modesty. A rally with a genteel admirer might have gone something like this. (All my father's comments are things he actually said about himself in print.)

> G.A.: *It is an honor to meet a man of such formidable accomplishment, Mr. Fadiman.*
> C.F.: *I have acquitted myself moderately well.*
> G.A.: *Moderately? Nonsense!*
> C.F.: *I have achieved a certain mild reputation as a wit.*
> G.A.: *But* Information Please *is incontestably brilliant!*
> C.F.: *I am master of a profession which in my more melancholy moments I range about midway between that of the bubblegum chewer and that of the bathroom baritone.*

G.A.: *What becoming humility! And in such a distin-
    guished man of letters!*

C.F.: *A rank amateur.*

G.A.: *Well, surely you must consider yourself a critic of
    the first rank.*

C.F.: *I suppose I have developed certain minor special-
    ized abilities, like a retriever or an aphid.*

And on and on and on, until the players ran out of shuttlecocks.

It could get tiresome. Jacques Barzun said that self-deprecation was my father's "one irritating trait."

And sometimes it was not an act. Beneath the posturing there lay a core of truth. If you scraped hard enough, some ugly things were laid bare: anxiety, humiliation, shame. It makes me uncomfortable to remember them. It makes me uncomfortable to name them.

11

Demeatballization

My father, of course, was happy that my brother and I went to Harvard. He once told me that boys from his own social class had not been able to lift their eyes that high. City College was the norm; Columbia was the hope; Harvard was, as he put it, "Camelot."

And I was happy there, surrounded by collegiate versions of the Gauloise-smoking Sartre-quoters I'd hung out with in France. Compared with my father, I had an easy path: no commuting by subway, no waiting tables, no breaking in pipes. Unlike his college friends, mine felt no obligation to choose between demolishing the establishment and joining the club; they protested the Vietnam War by day and read Dante Gabriel Rossetti in wood-paneled libraries by night. If they thought there was anything strange about a miniskirted girl from L.A. pronouncing *ar*istocrat and *ex*quisite with the stress on the first syllable (my father believed that anyone who said *ar*istocrat or ex*quis*ite was neither), they held their tongues, though my freshman roommate did once give me a funny look when I complimented her on her "stripèd socks."

My father visited frequently when he flew east from Los Angeles on what he called his "literary menstrual cycle" to attend meetings of the Book-of-the-Month Club, for which he had long served as a judge. He might not have been the ideal consort for the Father-Daughter Picnic, but he was a hit at Harvard. He was in his late sixties while Kim and I were in college, but our friends hardly seemed to notice his age, perhaps because he looked exactly like their gray-haired professors and yet, unlike the real ones, was always interested in what they had to say. The qualities that had made Dorothy Thompson call him her ideal dinner guest—wit, urbanity, the ability to quote a Wordsworth sonnet or compose a mildly bawdy limerick—played just as well thirty years later with a cast of students in frayed jeans.

When he came to Cambridge, he usually took us to a good restaurant along with a roommate or two, but once he threw a small party in a Harvard club. The occasion was a wine-and-cheese tasting to celebrate my brother's twenty-first birthday.

I volunteered to write the menu. Write it? I *calligraphed* it, using an italic pen I had been given in the eighth grade. Kim, unfortunately, saved the incriminating document.

Oh, how I blush to read it now. The pomposity of the crimson seal at the top of the Veritas stationery I had bought at the Harvard Coop! The earnest attempt at Gothic lettering, embellished with extra little serifs on

The Twenty-first Birthday of Kim Whitmore Fadiman
The Signet Club
15 April
1972

pâté de foie

~

Les Fromages:

le brie   le reblochon   le gruyère
     l'excelsior   le beaumont
          la crème danîa
          le boursault

~

Les Vins:

Sherry Royal Vintage 1862
Chateau Latour 1945   La Tâche 1947
          Romanee Conti 1934
          Port 1840
          (sans nom)

~

café   gaufrettes   noix

~

grand gateau de naissance

My menu for Kim's twenty-first birthday party, 1972

the *B*s, *F*s, *L*s, *V*s, and *W*s! The mislabeling of the venue, which was actually the Signet *Society*, not the Signet *Club*! The pretentious transposition of number and month in "15 April"! The scattershot accent marks! The off-key French, especially in the effort to designate the anonymous 1840 port, which I characterized as "*sans nom*"! What kind of girl would create such a document? Shall we just wring her neck?

But oh, how my father must have loved it all. The anachronistic formality of the gathering. The setting, a literary association to which George Santayana and T. S. Eliot had belonged. The leatherbound volumes on the shelves. The portraits of dead WASPs on the walls. The definitive demeatballization of his children.

He charmed, he scintillated, he educated. Latour is a great Bordeaux. La Tâche and Romanée-Conti are two great Burgundies. The vagaries of weather make some vintages especially fine, and we are fortunate to have three Great Years here: 1934, 1945, and 1947. We can still drink port and sherry from the nineteenth century because they are fortified wines, infused with brandy to halt fermentation.

Kim and I had heard about wines like these—the names were as familiar to us as Coke and Pepsi—but we had never tasted anything on their level. Our father had been saving them for this occasion. He had laid down the 1840 port (*sans nom*) when Kim was born. Their extravagance was, of course, preposterous. I knew that most families didn't live the way we did—there was, among other things, the matter of the cook, though he had been let go when I left for college—but we didn't ski at Gstaad or wear jewelry from Cartier or drive Rolls-Royces or . . . well, I wasn't sure what the superrich did, but we weren't them. We drove Buicks. We gave each other books for Christmas. We didn't usually serve refreshments that in a restaurant would have cost as much as several months of our Harvard tuition.

In addition to Kim, me, and our parents, there were, I think, six guests. Five of them couldn't have told a Romanée-Conti from a Chianti. They did their best to look appropriately pensive as they swirled their goblets and sniffed the bouquets—in the case of the port, a cloudlet of aromatic molecules that had been trapped in glass for more than a century.

The evening was our father's idea of what a twenty-first birthday party should be, not Kim's. The guest of honor enjoyed the cheese and the *grand gâteau de naissance*, but he remembers sensing a poignant gap between what he thought he should feel about the wines and what he actually felt. Like me, he had been steeped in oenophilia all his life. When he was a toddler, he had learned to identify liqueurs and fortified wines by smell and bottle shape; our father enjoyed wheeling his stroller into liquor stores, where, to their proprietors' amazement and dismay (bets were generally involved), the little genius unerringly chirped, as a procession of open bottles was placed before him, "Sherry . . . vermouth . . . crème de menthe . . . Falernum . . . Angostura bitters . . ." At Harvard, Kim had bought a set of wineglasses for his dormitory room and joined the Lowell House Wine-Tasting Society. But on his birthday he remembers saying to himself, "These are the great wines of the world and I am not getting anything from this experience." And that was that. From then on, he drank wine if it was served to him but never bought it and rarely talked about it.

For a long time, I thought of that evening as the Emperor's New Wine Tasting. I now realize it was the opposite. The emperor's clothes were real. The populace was blind.

The majority of the populace, that is. The sixth guest could not only appreciate *Les Vins* (as I had termed them on the menu) but appreciate them exquisitely. Kim's roommate, John Laird, was from Ohio, the son of a gas company executive who drank Scotch on the rocks; there was nothing in his background to explain why he loved wine. He just did, like a man who inexplicably loves philately or sports cars or jazz.

The summer after Kim's party, John worked as a sous-chef at a French restaurant on Cape Cod. At the end of August, he spent everything he'd earned on twenty-five cases of Burgundy and Bordeaux that he shipped to his parents' house in Columbus for safekeeping. The following year, when he was a senior, my father asked him, "What are you thinking of doing after college, John?"

"Gee, I don't know," he said. "My father wants me to go to law school."

"Well, you like wine," said my father. "There are people who make a living in the wine industry."

"They do?"

So John disappointed his own father and gratified mine. My father introduced him to Sam Aaron, Alexis Lichine, and Frank Schoonmaker, the three great lords of the American wine world. John ended up working for the first two, researching and ghostwriting their books before becoming something of a lord himself, the president of one of the most distinguished wine-importing companies in the world. He was the wine-progeny my father deserved.

John, by the way, did not think of that party as a wasteful casting of pearls before swine. He thought that whether or not everyone could appreciate the wines, it was an appropriate way to celebrate, through the medium my father held most dear, the coming-of-age of a beloved son.

And what of the insufferable calligrapher? What did she think of all this?

My memories of that evening are mostly fond. I remember being bemused—and perhaps confused—by the expense, which, though it was never mentioned, I could guess. But I liked being in a room with my brother and both of our parents. I felt my life before college and my life during college inching into alignment. When I had left home, the bookish vocabulary I had acquired at the Fadiman dinner table had been poured smoothly and usefully into the vessel of my literary studies, but there was nowhere to pour the wine vocabulary. It therefore felt deeply satisfying to write that ridiculous menu and to savor the names as they rolled off my father's tongue.

Yes, but what did I think of the *wines*?

"Think of the wines" is an appropriate phrase. I can say with accuracy that I thought about them. I liked the idea of them. But as for the taste of them, I remember absolutely nothing.

12

Milkshake

My father laid down a nineteenth-century port for the wine lover's son, but he did not lay down anything for the wine lover's daughter. I asked him about it once. He shrugged and said, "I was a male chauvinist. Kim was a male." He then told me he owed me a twenty-first birthday party, an offer that might have been more valuable if I hadn't been in my thirties when he made it.

He hadn't thrown an expensive party for my half brother, Jono, either. Jono—the son of the arduously retrieved Polly, so much older than I that he seemed a member of a different generation—had turned twenty-one when Kim was a toddler and my mother was pregnant with me. His coming-of-age had likely ceded precedence to the urgent demands of my father's new family. Still, there was something specifically gender-ish about the situation. My father *was* a male chauvinist.

He liked women—relished them, studied them, adored them. As a good progressive who would no sooner have glugged a Pétrus straight from the bottle than voted Republican, he supported the Equal Rights Amendment and called its defeat "the act of barbarians." But that didn't stop him from being reflexively condescending. I was recently trolling the online archives of *The New York Times* for articles that mentioned both "Clifton Fadiman" and "wine" (there were fifty-four) when I came upon an account of a talk he delivered on June 5, 1958, at the "21" Club, on the occasion of the Cigar Institute of America's Annual Ladies' Smoker. He asserted that although they were better drivers (true enough in his own household, since no one could have driven more incompetently than he did), "women are not as good at conversation and they know absolutely nothing about wine."

Oh God, here we go again. Reading about my father, I was always bumping into howlers like that. But this one achieved a hitherto unmatched level of brazenness: He didn't say it at a men's club, he said it at a *ladies' luncheon*. (If an unusual one. Were his listeners—who, according to the *Times* reporter, wore flowery hats—all puffing on coronas and panatelas while my father informed them of their inferiority in two of his most cherished spheres?)

It was the times, I reminded myself. The cigar-smoking ladies may have chuckled just as merrily as the female fans of *Information Please* undoubtedly did when he'd posed such questions (chosen by the producer, I hasten to note) as "Kipling said, 'The female of the species is more deadly than the male.' Can you quote two more selections that would please a woman-hater?" But even when those times were long past, he continued to make jokes about the bird-witted literary tastes of housewives; to call women "girls"; and, in both speech and writing, to use "he" when he meant "he or she." I'm sure he had lower expectations for his daughter than he did for his sons. This persistent bias, as immune to rehabilitation as his own fondness for cigars (the smellier the better), both devalued and protected me. It meant that the pressure fell more heavily on Kim, who, perhaps because his father so intensely wanted him to be a writer, became a wilderness instructor and commodities trader, and on Jono, who went into computer engineering and marketing, although now, in his eighties, he manages a bookstore—a more Fadimanian calling. The writer niche was left open for me.

A few years ago I read a book by Carolyn Heilbrun called *When Men Were the Only Models We Had*. It was about three of her mentors: my father and his two closest college friends, Jacques Barzun and Lionel Trilling. Barzun and Trilling taught Heilbrun at Columbia before she became a professor there herself; she included my father in her trio, even though she'd never met him, because, she explained, "Fadiman's was the life I thought I might live, his the writing that suggested how I might myself one day write." When she was fifteen, she had come across *Reading I've Liked*—an anthology prefaced by an autobiographical essay in which my father traced the arc of his reading history from *The Overall Boys*, perused at age four, to the books he reviewed for *The New Yorker* in his thirties—and vowed to become "a Fadiman." By this she meant a writer who was "both intellectual, even 'highbrow,' and yet available to those who did not think of themselves as either." All three icons ended up tumbling off their pedestals when Heilbrun realized, in her forties, that their attitudes toward women ranged from discomfort with gender parity to outright misogyny. Her feminist rapier found its mark with particular exactitude when she turned to my father and, citing chapter and verse, observed that "magically, when he reaches for a sorry example of writing, behold, a woman writer he finds at his fingertips." Though her book was a model of the sort of accessible intellectualism she had admired as a teenager—she *did* become a Fadiman—I can hardly say I enjoyed it. (Like boys who fight with their brothers at home but defend them from bullies at school, children always feel they're the only ones who have the right to criticize their parents.) But I had to admit that Heilbrun was right.

My father believed there were certain things only a man should do. Earn more than his spouse. Pay the check at a restaurant. Hold the tickets at an airport. Be the last through a door. Tell the taxi driver where to go. Repeat an off-color joke.

And, of course, swear. Vladimir Nabokov, one of his favorite writers, described his own father, a patrician Russian statesman, as dignified in public but ribald in private. So too my father. In his eyes, swearing was not vulgar; it was a manly prerogative, as long as it was never done in writing or within earshot of children. Incorporating an occasional mild obscenity—"screw" or "balls," for instance, but never "fuck"—into conversation with his offspring was a way of welcoming us into adulthood. (Some families might observe this rite of passage by serving wine, but of course we had passed that milestone long ago.) These words were reserved for him and for my brothers, though both of them spurned the privilege and spoke as chastely as nuns. My father believed it was appropriate for women to hear salty language but not to use it. When he told me something was horseshit, that was a token of fond familiarity. But had I responded in kind, he would have raised his eyebrows, which were gray and curly and had occasional rogue hairs that snaked out at peculiar angles.

My father also believed that, as a general rule, women were more superficial thinkers than men. How could they not be, with so much of their mental effort siphoned off to dresses, hats, and where to put the sofa? However, he was willing to make exceptions of the some-of-my-best-friends-are-Jews variety. It would have been hard not to, given that he had married my mother.

Although she had more than a passing interest in dresses, hats, and sofa placement, my mother was the antithesis of a fluffhead. Unlike many men who condescend to women, my father would never have chosen a dumb wife. Had he merely wanted a class-vaulting accessory, he would have plucked a WASP from the New York Social Register—plenty would have been glad to oblige—rather than falling for a WASP-Mormon-agnostic from Utah. He was pleased, however, that Annalee Whitmore Jacoby was what he called "well bred" (by which he meant she wasn't Jewish and she hadn't grown up poor, at least not until her banker father lost most of his money before the Depression and the rest during it; he viewed her as akin to a Chekhovian aristocrat who had been forced to live in reduced circumstances). He envied her social ease, an insider's natural right rather than an outsider's acquired skill. She added a few squiggles to his arrow-straight trajectory. If she'd been a wine, she would have been not a first-growth French Bordeaux but one of the best of the new California wines that had cropped up since Prohibition—say, an Inglenook Cabernet, a fine varietal in the vernacular style.

I once asked him why he had married her. He told me that she had a superior mind, she foamed with liveliness, and she looked irresistible in a white silk Chinese dress that was extremely sexy even though it buttoned all the way up to her neck. He added, "And both of us were looking for something because each of us had suffered. In your mother's case it was a real tragedy, and in mine it was a pretty bad trauma." He meant the unraveling of his marriage to Polly.

My mother's summary of the situation was that when she compared my father with his potential rivals, "he made the other ones look like palookas."

Up to that point, my mother had made a career of confounding feminine stereotypes. She was the first woman managing editor of *The Stanford Daily*; one of the few women who rose from the stenography pool to become a screenwriter at MGM, where she co-wrote scripts for movies starring Judy Garland, Mickey Rooney, Lana Turner, and Clark Gable; as a reporter for Time-Life, the only woman war correspondent in China. I once wrote a piece of celebratory doggerel about her that included these lines:

> *She sailed off to China in the heat of the war,*
> *With MacArthur and Stilwell she forged a rapport,*
> *And while dining on mule meat and K-ration mousse*
> *She sent daily dispatches to Henry R. Luce.*
> *She returned with a knowledge of Rolleiflex optics,*
> *She could type under fire and eat ice cream with*
>   *chopsticks—*
> *But I think that what really brought Kip to his knees*
> *Was the fact that my mother could curse in Chinese.*

(It was apparently permissible for women to swear in languages he didn't understand.)

The tragedy to which my father referred was the loss of her first husband, a journalist named Melville Jacoby who died in a military accident six months after their wedding in Manila and two months after the newlyweds escaped from Corregidor. Not long before she met my father, she collaborated on a book with Theodore H. White, the self-described meatball who went on to become a well-known political reporter. *Thunder Out of China*, an angry critique of America's Far East policy, became a bestseller and was banned both in China and in U.S. State Department libraries. My mother and Teddy, who had long been in love with her and had tendered an

My mother working on a script at MGM, circa 1940

unsuccessful proposal, were invited to be guest panelists on *Information Please*. Oscar Levant told my father he should marry her.

He seems to have needed little encouragement. He courted my mother by buying her a flamethrower to melt the snow in her driveway (on the assumption, I feel sure, that *she* would be the one to use it) and by once bringing her a large quantity of a rum cocktail of which he was especially proud and which went over so well that both she and her mother got, as he recalled it, "tight as ticks." (My mother remembered the drink as an alcoholic milkshake, which may have been more likely, since, like me, she was very fond of milkshakes. Either way, you will note that he didn't bring wine. Too la-di-da. He had figured out that pretension, which had served him well ever since he left Brooklyn, would get him nowhere with a woman who had been dodging bombs in Chungking while he was exchanging *bons mots* in Upper East Side salons.) When I observed that getting my mother drunk might have had certain advantages but that it seemed unnecessary to get my grandmother drunk as well, my father insisted that the intention in both cases had been entirely innocent.

I am every bit as much the milkshake lover's daughter as I am the wine lover's daughter. My mother provided many things my father couldn't: comparative youth (she was twelve years his junior); an easy rapport with my middle-school friends (if there had been a *Mother-*Daughter Picnic, I would have brought her); an appreciation for all-American pleasures like root beer and the Academy Awards (from her days on the MGM lot, she knew lots of gossip about the older actors); a matter-of-fact attitude toward sex and bodily functions (on a European trip with our father while Kim and I were at summer camp, she mailed us variously textured samples of toilet paper, one from each city, for our amusement and cultural edification); a love of nature (on Florida vacations, she organized midnight expeditions to stinky mudflats where, flashlights in hand, we patrolled the sand for king's crown conchs while our father lay in bed, reading Book-of-the-Month Club galleys). When he was out of town, she took us to Shakey's, where we listened to honky-tonk piano and ate pizza, a food he reviled, both because it was eaten with the hands (vulgar and unsanitary) and because it contained garlic (vulgar and foul-tasting). She was less worried about money. She didn't put herself down.

But when I addressed my letters from Paris to The Clifton Fadimans, I may have been onto more than I knew. Marriage and children effaced my mother's former self, or at least the part that had thumbed its nose at conventional gender roles. She missed the career she had given up—by her own choice, in the sneakily cruel manner of those prefeminist times, which arranged things so that there was no one to blame but yourself, though you ended up blaming your husband anyway. In the early years of their marriage, she spent a lot of time giving dinner parties for my father's friends and typing the scripts for the shows he hosted, first on radio, then on television. (Her days in the MGM steno pool had left her with crackerjack secretarial skills.) Although my father participated with greater enthusiasm than most men of his era in the more congenial aspects of parenthood, such as making up stories about bibliophilic worms, she was the one who drove us to school, buckled our galoshes, and coaxed foul-tasting medicines down our throats when we had earaches. Interviewers—invariably his, though she had once had plenty of her own—referred to her, if they mentioned her work at all, as "a newshen," "an authoress," and "as pretty a gal correspondent as ever strummed a portable." Even when she was in her seventies, a reporter remarked that she was "cute as a bug's navel."

Within my parents' imperfect but interesting marriage, wine was always an area of accord. Having wooed her with rum cocktails (or milkshakes), my father successfully introduced her to wine, which she enjoyed in a cheerful, unassuming, nothing-to-prove way. They shared at least a half bottle, and for many years a full one, every night with dinner. My mother was no connoisseur, but it is true that she once told him, after they drank a La Tâche '49 as guests of his old college friend Mortimer Adler—who had become, as my father approvingly put it, "the only practicing philosopher in history able to make money in respectable quantities"—that it was the best wine she had ever tasted. In fact, at my brother's twenty-first birthday party, it is entirely possible that my father and John Laird were not the only ones who could appreciate the La Tâche '47, not to mention the Romanée-Conti '34, the Latour '45, the Sherry Royal Vintage 1862, and the Port 1840 (*sans nom*).

13

Jew

Earlier in these pages, I enumerated the reasons why my father loved wine. Here is one more: Wine wasn't Jewish.

I have rarely mentioned to a Jew that I was writing about my father and wine without being told, "Of course, Jews don't drink!"—an observation often tendered as said Jew raises his or her glass of wine in mock-toast. One friend told me that whenever a relative drinks too much champagne at a wedding, her family calls him Joe Goy. Another, a klezmer musician, said, "Right! Shiker iz der goy."

"What?"

"'*Shiker Iz der Goy*.' It's a famous Yiddish folk song. It means 'The Gentile Is Drunk.'"

I found it later in a book called *Tenement Songs: The Popular Music of the Jewish Immigrants*, a title my father would never have wanted on his shelves. Here is a translation of the first two verses:

The gentile goes into the tavern.
He drinks a glass of wine there.
Oy, the gentile is drunk.
He's drunk, he has to drink,
Because he's a gentile.

The Jew goes into the house of study.
He looks into a book there.
Oy, the Jew is sober.
He's sober, he has to study,
Because he's a Jew.

In other words, if you drink a glass of wine, you can't be Jewish. Q.E.D.

To my father, it didn't matter whether this was true, just whether it was perceived as true. And the perception was that Jews knew nothing about wine. If they drank at all, they drank Manischewitz. The only wine he ever unequivocally dissed in print was "a certain beverage that advertises itself on the car cards and subway posters of New York City as 'the wine you can cut with a knife.'" He called it "bottled syrup." He did not name the syrup, but why was I not surprised to find out that it was Schapiro's Kosher Wine, pressed from sweet Concord grapes in the basement of a tenement on the Lower East Side?

When I was growing up, the whole idea of Jewishness was deeply mysterious. I was brought up in a household so nonreligious (not *anti*religious, since religion was never criticized, merely absent) that I resembled a child who

has been raised in an excessively antiseptic environment—
Lysol on the counters, Phisohex on the hands—and has
therefore developed no immunities. My mother was of
Scots Presbyterian stock with more recent ancestral detours
into Mormonism, but the operative fact was that, like my
father, she was an agnostic. (They weren't atheists. That
would have betrayed their shared commitment to ratio-
nality, since how could you know for sure?) My father
once wrote that he was so devoid of religious feeling that
"it is as though the Great Monosyllable were a nonsense
word, like xbyabt." The only vaguely pious term he ever
used was "Blessings," the last word he said whenever he
bade farewell to a family member. But it was always clear
that *he* was the one doing the blessing.

If xbyabt was not immanent in our home, neither was
much sense of identification with our father's branch of
the family. Our mother could talk for hours about her
ancestors, chief among them the great-grandfather who
traveled to Utah in a wagon train, maintained three wives
in three separate households, and at one point had thirteen children under the age of fourteen. She could have
drawn a verdant family tree. Our father told us amusing
stories about growing up in Brooklyn; his humble beginnings were an important part of his self-deprecatory ar-
senal. Like James Thurber's winsomely baroque family
of flakes and screwballs, the relatives who were part of
his childhood were comic fodder: the cousin who could
read at age three and had a nervous breakdown at twenty-
five; the uncle who was 4'7" (though my father once
admitted, "I think I was being malicious when I told you

that—he was four eight easy"). But on the rare occasions when his more distant family history came up, he knew few details and, as far as I could see, had little desire to learn more. He once mentioned that three of his aunts had been killed by Cossacks in a pogrom, but he didn't know their names. He didn't even know the names of his grandparents. How could anyone not know that?

His parents had been freethinkers, mildly socialist and strongly secular. I asked him once if his family had celebrated Hanukkah, and he looked at me as if I had asked whether they had eaten raccoons. Jewish parents who name their sons Edwin, Clifton, and William are conveying a pretty clear message.

My maternal grandmother—a retired librarian whose uncle had been the mayor of Salt Lake City—lived near us and was my favorite babysitter, but my paternal grandparents hovered on the remotest periphery of my consciousness. Bettemi, who had taken the goyish name Grace after her marriage, died before I was born. Isadore lived until I was ten, but I met him only once. I'm sure my father was ashamed of his father's accent, his lack of education, his proletarian manners, his palpable Jewishness. And where had he learned shame? From his father. Whenever Grace spoke Yiddish, Isadore had winced; he considered it inferior to Russian, which he spoke well and she spoke poorly. The Fadimans had fashioned a little daisy chain of shame: The father was ashamed of the wife and the son was ashamed of the father, though the only one who was ashamed of the son was himself.

I don't remember hearing the phrase "bat mitzvah"

until I was well beyond bat mitzvah age. At school, my class of sixty had 1.5 Jews; the .5 was not chummy with the 1. When I was invited to a Shabbat dinner by a girl I had met through my YMCA group—it had attempted to foster ecumenical sisterhood by introducing the Christians (us) to some teenagers from a local synagogue (them)— the noodle kugel seemed far more exotic than the Rumaki Puu Puu served at the Islander, a "Polynesian" restaurant on La Cienega, disdained by our father but beloved by the rest of the family, that featured fake thunderstorms every hour. When Kim and I were told we were going to have a new tennis instructor, I had no idea that it was because the old one, doubtless chosen by our mother, worked at a Jewish country club, and the new one, doubt-less chosen by our father, worked at a gentile club. In the larger world, I could never tell who was Jewish. Aside from names—names were easy, they were *words*—I couldn't even begin to guess what kinds of cues other people's ra-dar picked up. When I read *Hamlet* in twelfth grade, I remember asking myself: What about Rosencrantz and Guildenstern? They sound Jewish, but they can't be! Or can they? Is there such a thing as a Jewish Dane? Are they wicked and foolish because Shakespeare was an anti-Semite, and if so, does everybody know that but me?

A cousin of mine once hired a researcher in Minsk to look into the Fadiman genealogy and learned that for three generations in what is now Belarus, our ancestors were named either Fadiman or Fodiman, which seem to have been used interchangeably. (I was disappointed. I had hoped that my real name had at least five syllables, something along the lines of Feydimanovsky.) My father was undoubtedly grateful that his last name was ethnically ambiguous. He didn't have to anglicize or shorten it, unlike some of his friends and their families. George Novack was once Yasef Mendel Novograbelsky; Felix Morrow was once Felix Mayrowitz. Diana Trilling tells the story of the Columbia philosophy professor who made a pointed comment about Morrow's distinguished last name. "I wouldn't know about that," Morrow replied pleasantly. "I'm the first in my family to bear it."

In the early 1970s, the writer David Wallace, the son of my father's friend Irving Wallace, went in the other direction and changed his name to David Wallechinsky, his family's original name. My father thought this was lunatic. Roots were for cutting off, not for reattaching. Who in his right mind would *choose* to be named Wallechinsky? At the time I thought his sputterings were hilarious, but I now see that they had a sharp edge. He was angry at David for thumbing his nose at the pain his father's generation—*my* father's generation—had suffered.

Much has been written about the anti-Semitism of gentiles in the first half of the twentieth century, but not so much about the self-alienation of Jews—not all, not even the majority, but a large number of secular intellectuals that included my father and many of his friends. It led to such farcical moments as my father telling Diana Trilling, when they were reminiscing about a literary magazine to which both he and Lionel had contributed,

"I don't think we thought of it as a Jewish journal." They were talking about *The Menorah Journal*. This was like saying they didn't think of *Canoe & Kayak* as a magazine about boats. Lionel once declared in the *Contemporary Jewish Record*, "I know of no writer in English who has added a micromillimeter to his stature by 'realizing his Jewishness.'" Today this sounds like denial bordering on paranoia, but whenever I have the urge to go back in time and tell them to knock it off, I remind myself that I don't have a clue what they were up against and never will.

At the turn of the twentieth century, fewer than 10 percent of Columbia's students were Jews. By the time my father arrived at Columbia in 1920, the figure had risen to 40 percent. I learned this only recently, and it surprised me: I had always assumed his circle was a small, beleaguered minority. I was wrong about the small part. Columbia had more Jews than any other Ivy League school because it was in New York City, into which, starting in the 1880s, hundreds of thousands of immigrants had poured. This was a problem, because Jews—especially Eastern European Jews, my father's strain, as compared with German Jews, who were considered more cultivated—were viewed as uncouth strivers with iffy personal hygiene and the potential, as Columbia's dean put it, of making the university "socially uninviting to students who come from homes of refinement." (The dean was careful to add that after a generation or two in adequate social surroundings, Jews could become "entirely satisfactory companions.")

A fraternity song from the 1910s went like this:

Oh, Harvard's run by millionaires
And Yale is run by booze
Cornell is run by farmers' sons
Columbia's run by Jews.

A later verse contained the lines "And when the little sheenies die / Their souls will go to hell."

The challenge was where they went *before* they died—specifically, when they were around eighteen years old. How could they be discreetly steered away from Morningside Heights, to which the subway so conveniently led from the Lower East Side and Brooklyn? Columbia's president, Nicholas Murray Butler, had a few ideas. Starting in 1919, he required applicants to state their religious affiliation, specify their father's birthplace, and submit a photograph. He introduced non-academic criteria—including "straightforwardness," "clean-mindeness," "public spirit," and "geographical range," along with a psychological examination designed to winnow out swots whose ambition exceeded their "native intelligence"—that allowed the university more wiggle room in its admissions decisions. His new dean wrote, "We have honestly attempted to eliminate the lowest grade of applicant and it turns out that a good many of the low grade men are New York City Jews." Two years after my father arrived, the proportion of Jews in the incoming class had been successfully reduced to 22 percent. If he had been two years younger, would he have been admitted? Or would he have ended up at City College (more than 80 percent Jewish)?

No matter how brilliant they were, my father and his circle could not shrug off the label. When he was in his seventies, he sent me a 1927 essay by Mark Van Doren called "Jewish Students I Have Known." It was a series of sketches of seven undergraduates, referred to by letters, whom Van Doren had recently taught at Columbia. In an accompanying note, my father provided a key:

A = Henry Rosenthal
B = Clifton Fadiman
C = Meyer Schapiro
D = John Gassner
E = Herbert Solow
F = Lionel Trilling
G = Charles Prager

C was erudite and loquacious, F fastidious and melancholy. B was worldly and amusing, a gifted mimic with a mischievous tongue and the air of having read everything ever written. "His tongue did not wait to strike; it was always playing," wrote Van Doren. "B could adjust himself to any condition. He could pick up any extra money he needed; he could impress any superior; he could write on any subject." (In his note, my father observed, "The portrait of me is inaccurate in many respects. Mark did not see that I was scared, impractical, sentimental. Which, of course, I still am.") There is not a single negative word in Van Doren's essay, but reading it is an odd experience.

It's like a field guide to an exotic but unappreciated bird species compiled by an ornithologist who is highly pleased with himself for noticing identifying features (iridescent plumage! forked tail! curved beak!) that others have overlooked.

When Van Doren's birds were at Columbia, there were four Jewish faculty members. Jews were viewed as clever and industrious, but their brand of diligence (a trait one Harvard observer called "underliving and overworking") was not what Ivy League humanities departments were looking for. How could an uncultured person transmit culture? In New Haven, an aspiring English professor was informed, "Mr. Cohen, you are a very competent young man, but it is hard for me to imagine a Hebrew teaching the Protestant tradition to young men at Yale." (Elliot Cohen managed to dust himself off and become the founding editor of *Commentary*.) It was said that another Mr. Cohen—a philosopher named Morris who ended up at City College—was turned down for a Yale position because he did not know how to wear a dinner jacket.

My father, who had overworked but not underlived and, by the time he finished college, probably knew how to wear a dinner jacket, started graduate school at Columbia with the hope of being appointed to the English faculty, which (in the words of Alfred Kazin, a City College man) was "as crowded with three-barreled Anglican names as the House of Bishops": Harry Morgan Ayres, Jefferson Butler Fletcher, George Philip Knapp, William Witherle Lawrence, George Dinsmore Odell, William Peterfield

Trent. Joining them would allow my father to spend the rest of his life studying literature, the only thing he loved as much as wine. It would also constitute the ultimate proof that he had crossed the river.

One day the head of the department informed him, "We have room for only one Jew, and we have chosen Mr. Trilling."

My father never got over that moment. Many years later, he wrote that he had always dreamed of being "a scholar, perhaps even a college professor" but had instead ended up in "activities that have resulted in my becoming a kind of hemi-demi-semi-professor, or perhaps only a hemi-demi-semi-quasi-professor." Because he made more money and became more famous than any professor, his readers doubtless assumed that this was just another volley of false self-deprecation. It wasn't. He said he lacked the brains, but the real reason he didn't get the job was that he lacked the pedigree.

Mr. Trilling went on to become one of the great literary scholars of the twentieth century; my father went on to become, in Dwight Macdonald's view, a middlebrow who, along with Thornton Wilder, John Steinbeck, Archibald MacLeish, *Harper's*, *The Atlantic*, and psychoanalysis, polluted modern America with the "tepid ooze of Midcult." Mr. Trilling taught university students; in his twenties, my father taught salesgirls, stenographers, truck drivers, merchant seamen, night watchmen, and clerks in the Great Books classes he led in libraries and YMCAs, and, later on, millions of Americans who read his essays and reviews and forewords and afterwords and anthologies, or listened to him on the radio, or watched him on television, or heard his intermission lectures at the Boston Symphony, or subscribed to the Book-of-the-Month Club. What Ed had done for him by making him read an entire college literature textbook at the age of thirteen, he did for the general public. Although middlebrows considered him a highbrow, highbrows disowned him. Jacques Barzun loyally argued that my father's career was a noble crusade to civilize the philistines, though his defense shone with a little too much sweat; he had to admit that, as he put it, "popularity was the fatal stain." My father couldn't have guessed that the young Mr. Trilling so grievously envied his early fame as a critic that he became discouraged about his own prospects; Diana Trilling believed this contributed to a severe depression during which he lied to her about working on his dissertation when he was really spending his days at the movies. But Mr. Trilling never envied my father as much as my father envied him.

None of this would have happened if my father had been born an Episcopalian.

So I believed him when he told me that of all the factors that made him feel like an outsider—being poor, being short, having parents who spoke improper English, having an elder brother he thought he could never equal—the most important was being a Jew. He said, without irony, that he was certain all Jews felt like that: Jewish governors, Jewish millionaires. He once told Kim that whenever he looked at a page in a book or a newspaper, the capital *J*s—which he reflexively assumed were attached to the word "Jew"—immediately leapt to his eye, "the way I might spot my own initials." He also told Kim that after he revisited one of his old neighborhoods in Brooklyn, "I was right back there. I was a little Jew boy walking the streets of Brooklyn, and I still am."

My college boyfriend was half-Jewish, like me, but his longest-running successor (until I met my husband) was an alumnus of Groton who bore the almost parodically WASP name of Sedgwick and would someday rest in a circular cemetery plot in Stockbridge, Massachusetts, called the Sedgwick Pie, with his feet pointed toward the center, where his great-great-great-grandfather was buried. It was said that the deceased Sedgwicks were oriented this way so that when they rose on Judgment Day, they would see no one but other Sedgwicks.

"Do they mind that you're a half Jew?" my father asked me once.

I explained that "they" had already managed to absorb *entire* Jews. He seemed unconvinced.

Now I think he wasn't worrying about what the Sedgwicks would think of me; he was worrying about what I would think of myself. I'm sure he wanted me to marry a WASP—where else was my demeatballization supposed to lead?—but not *that* much of a WASP. (I did end up marrying a WASP, though not a Sedgwick. The Colts don't have a pie-shaped cemetery. Also, George doesn't look like a WASP. When he was young he was told he resembled Bob Dylan; when he was older, Philip Roth.) My father feared that if I entered the Sedgwick family, the curtain would fall away, and all the things he'd worked so hard to make me feel were naturally and deservedly mine—the big house, the private schools, the fine restaurants, the French accent, the cook summoned by the buzzer over my mother's knee—would be revealed as fraudulent, the rightful province only of people who had enjoyed them for generations. In fact, though the Sedgwicks had an even bigger house, it was scruffier than ours, and though they had a cook until their youngest child left for boarding school, she served dinner at the kitchen table. The Fadimans had overdone it. On Judgment Day, when the Sedgwicks rose from the Pie, I'd be unmasked.

When I wrote the *Life* story about my father's eightieth birthday, he told me that he would prefer I not mention he was Jewish. "If I had no legs and you wrote a piece about me," he said, "I would prefer you write about me as a man."

I gaped at him. "I don't feel that being a Jew is equivalent to having no legs," I said.

My father didn't believe me. He simply could not imagine a time when being a Jew, or even a half Jew, was not a disability.

It was safer to raise his children so they could pass.

It was better to lay down a dozen cases of first-growth Bordeaux, because each one brought him closer to something he could never reach, but in whose direction, like a plant bending toward the sun, he could still turn. *Shiker iz der goy.*

14

Oakling

A few years ago I wrote an essay about Hartley Coleridge, a nineteenth-century British poet who had the bad luck to be the son of a far more famous poet, Samuel Taylor Coleridge. Hartley started off as a celebrated wunderkind and ended up a penniless alcoholic who often spent his days in alehouses and his nights in ditches. A review of the only book of Hartley's poetry published in his lifetime allowed that it manifested "no trivial inheritance of his father's genius"—a sincere compliment, if one that implied he had no genius of his own—but also cited an old adage: "The oakling withers beneath the shadow of the oak."

I am interested in oaklings because I am one myself. When writers beget writers, there are, of course, some advantages. There are plenty of books in the house. There's an example right under your nose that words are a plausible way to earn a living. There's the intimacy that comes when you and your parent like the same things and are both good at them.

There's also the likelihood that if you have at least semi-famous parents, you'll occasionally meet at least semi-famous people. My parents were hardly the L.A. equivalent of the Barzun *salonniers*, but one evening, at age eight, wearing a full-skirted organdy dress with appliquéd flowers, I opened the front door for Groucho Marx, a guest at the only genuinely flashy party they ever threw. A few years later, when my father interviewed P. L. Travers for a book he was writing on children's literature, I poured her tea. (The tea set was Victorian silver, bought in England, formerly the property of an earl who had fallen down on his luck: an anti-samovar.) The only thing I remember her saying is that William Butler Yeats had once chased her around a table; she did not say whether he caught her. When I was in college, my father and I had dinner at Julia Child's house in Cambridge. In one of his essays, he quotes Hilaire Belloc: "I cannot remember the name of the village; I do not even recollect the name of the girl; but the wine, my God, was Chambertin!" I, by contrast, remember the pegboard on the wall, the wooden slab wedged over the sink to conceal the dirty dishes, the wipeable Marimekko tablecloth, the horsey laugh, and the perfect roast chicken, but I do not remember the wine.

Despite the perks, oaklings face a universally acknowledged problem: the mighty oak grabs all the sunlight. One solution is relocating yourself as far as possible from the shadow. As I've mentioned, my brother and my half brother chose not to become writers. When Kim became an expert on avalanche prediction and Jono compiled a 204-page handbook on the circuitry of an early transistor-based computer called the Lincoln TX-2, they could rest assured that they were doing something their father could never have done. They were thereby saved the angst of Nick Harkaway, John le Carré's youngest son, who said that becoming a writer would feel as pointless as standing next to a lighthouse and waving a flashlight. He became one anyway.

Harkaway had only one lighthouse to worry about. I had two. (Plus a formidable older brother. Until our paths diverged after college, Kim was my Ed. He did all the same things I did—got good grades, backpacked, canoed, went to Harvard, majored in History and Literature—but a little sooner and a little better.) Fortunately, both had dimmed somewhat by the time I tentatively raised my own flashlight, which nonetheless felt like a tiny toy powered by a single AAA battery. I doubt I would have had the nerve to wave it at all had my mother not abandoned her career, conveniently situating her successes at a safe distance, or had my father not been so old. His age—something I once viewed as a liability—turned out to be a boon. My friends' parents had heard of him, but my friends hadn't, except perhaps as the genial but mildly fuddy-duddy host of the *Encyclopædia Britannica* films they had been required to watch in high school English class: a peripheral character who lacked the gleam of an authentic celebrity.

Still, he was famous enough that when I was starting out as a writer, I briefly considered using the name Anne Whitmore (I figured my mother's maiden name was safely forgotten) so that no one would compare Fadiman *père* and Fadiman *fille* or assume I was trading on my father's reputation. I gave up the idea only because it seemed unfair. I *was* Anne Fadiman. Why should I have to pretend to be someone else?

In my early twenties, I lived in an apartment with an editorial-assistant roommate, hundreds of cockroaches, a kitchen window with a missing pane, and a rent of which my share was $162.50 a month. This situation, I felt, was appropriate to my station as a freelancer, and it even had a certain romance: the Manhattan equivalent of a Parisian garret. I boxed up my mortifyingly unbohemian memories of being raised in a house with a uniformed cook. I was glad that my parents lived three thousand miles away, and that their image of where I lived, what I ate, what I drank, how I worked, and with whom I slept was as indistinct as a distant galaxy glimpsed through a child's telescope.

All the same, I had to admit that a little parental encouragement was not entirely unwelcome. "Anne lives in New York," my father wrote to an old friend, "trying to establish herself as the writer she essentially is. So far the path has been difficult, impeded by the emotional and romantic problems proper to her age. With a little luck, she may be heard from in the future." Not quite the panegyric he lavished in the same paragraph on Kim, whose career as an outdoor instructor was, he said, "a strange turn for a son of mine who is twice as intelligent as I am, three times the writer, and *n* times handsomer"—but nonetheless a plug, if a modest one, by someone solidly in my corner.

After I started writing full-time for *Life*, I worried that I might be suspected of benefiting from my parents' help and bent over backwards to make sure they didn't contribute so much as a semicolon. I rarely showed them my work before it was finished, lest they make a suggestion I actually wanted to use. But they read every piece after it was published, and my father unfailingly wrote me a letter of unconditional, and frequently unmerited, praise: a far cry from his famously acerbic *New Yorker* reviews, since he believed his children were a protected species and therefore warranted a suspension of his critical faculties. He also took pains to compliment me implicitly by asking my advice on the contents of his anthologies ("If you have a spare 3/4 of an hour, would you read 3 short stories by Sean O'Faolain and tell me which you like best?") and discussing literature (one letter mentioned, in this order and over the course of twelve paragraphs, Helprin, Tolstoy, Mann, Hemingway, Frost, Leithauser, Vonnegut, Barthelme, Mailer, Ginsberg, Didion, Montaigne, Chekhov, Roth, Malamud, Goethe, Céline, Beckett, Updike, Cheever, Byron, Kerouac, Kesey, Wolfe, Johnson, Savage, Goldsmith, Shakespeare, Keats, Baudelaire, Rimbaud, Joyce, Proust, Eliot, Yeats, Burroughs, Wallace, Michener, Uris, and Krantz).

Because he spent most of his time at his desk, a steel hulk with a surface area of eighteen square feet that exerted the gravitational pull of a small planet, he derived a

In my office at Life, *1984*

good deal of vicarious pleasure when I traveled. Once, when I was contemplating a reporting trip to Mauritius, he sent me the following:

> *On the island of Mauritius*
> *You will eat exotic dishes,*
> *All varieties of fishes,*
> *Thirteen different kinds of knishes,*
> *And (especially delicious)*
> *Shish kebab and other shishes.*
> *You'll fare well, with my best wishes,*
> *If you journey to Mauritius.*

This is, incidentally, the only time I remember him ever recommending a Jewish food. Those knishes would never have been allowed in had it not been for the rhyme scheme.

The classic oakling problem is that it is hard to become one's own person when that person so closely resembles someone else's person. There were, of course, a few areas in which my father and I diverged. He was a critic; I was a journalist. He had meticulous work habits; I was a procrastinator. He was neat; I was messy. His idea of recreation was reading in an armchair with his back to the window; I preferred climbing glaciers. He was unable to boil an egg; I enjoyed folding whipped cream into chocolate mousse and pummeling veal cutlets with a mallet. He had a hazy relationship with visual details and once, not insultingly, referred to a green skirt I was wearing as "some kind of bluish rag"; I could distinguish a red-tailed hawk from a sharp-shinned hawk by its flight pattern. He thought pets were boring, because they couldn't talk; at parties, I often spent more time with the dog than with the host.

But I had to admit that our similarities far outnumbered our differences. We were not only both writers but both devotees of Vermeer, late bedtimes, anagrams, and doggerel, which we often composed for family celebrations. When we took the Johnson O'Connor aptitude tests, we both scored in the "95th++" percentile (95 was the official maximum) in English Vocabulary and the 6th percentile in Lefthanded Finger Dexterity. We both loved pasta, cheese, and lamb chops; we both hated pickles, mayonnaise, and garnishes. I shared his horror when Sam Aaron took us to the Quilted Giraffe, an Upper East

Side restaurant whose very name represented everything my father detested about *nouvelle cuisine*, and he spied an ostensibly ornamental fragment of lettuce in the butter dish. "It is a travesty," he said, "to take a nice natural product and drape it with a disgusting piece of vegetable material, moist and horrible."

As oaks and oaklings are wont to do, we even looked alike. Our type was minutely described in 1825 by Brillat-Savarin, the French epicure who not only was one of our favorite writers but had lent his name to one of our favorite cheeses, a triple-crème with a fluffy white rind and a ravishingly unctuous interior. "People predestined to gourmandism," he wrote, "are in general of medium height; they have round or square faces, bright eyes, small foreheads, short noses, full lips and rounded chins." Aside from the small foreheads—and the medium height, which might be stretching things a little—that was us to a T. I should explain that to Brillat-Savarin, calling someone a gourmand was the highest of compliments. He pitied those who took little pleasure from eating: poor souls with long faces, long noses, and attenuated physiques. "It is undoubtedly they who invented trousers," he observed, "to hide their thin shanks." No thin-shank problem for us Fadimans!

You will notice that much of the large overlapping center of the father-daughter Venn diagram involved food. It was no accident that my father's poem about Mauritius was entirely about comestibles, right down to the shishes. In matters of gourmandism, the oakling was the spitting image of the oak. If I opened my refrigerator and spotted an unfinished pint of Haägen-Dazs, the butt end of a salami, or a fractional wheel of couldn't-afford-it-but-bought-it-anyway Brillat-Savarin, the doomed remnant would have little chance of lasting until the next day, or even the next ten minutes.

In the gastronomic realm, the only area of marked disagreement was the one in which I wished we were more similar. If I found half a bottle of wine left over from dinner with friends—or even some uncorked champagne carried home from a party, wreathed in convivial associations—it would languish for weeks. The champagne would go flat. The wine would turn to vinegar.

It's not that I disliked the taste of wine, exactly. It's that there was too *much* taste. Wine tasted to me sort of the way hard liquor (which I liked even less) must taste to most people—not bad, but better when diluted with club soda or Coke. I liked food *cooked* with wine; in fact, if I remembered that half bottle in the fridge before it oxidized into oblivion, I'd happily dump it into a pot of *coq au vin*. Once the alcohol boiled off, everything was fine—but that was like saying ice cream would be fine if you removed the cream. According to Charles Lamb, another writer of whom my father and I were jointly fond, "There is a smoothness and oiliness in wine that makes it go down by a natural channel, which I am positive was made for that descending." (Lamb wrote those words the day after so much wine descended his natural channel that he had to be carried home on a servant's shoulders, "like a dead log.") But wine didn't taste smooth and oily to me; it tasted astringent. I was more like Art Buchwald, who was once invited on a tour of great Bordeaux vineyards by Alexis Lichine. First they visited Château Margaux, where he said the wine tasted like cotton. Then they visited Château Latour, where, after a single sip, he said, "My mouth is all puckered up. My cheeks are stuck to my teeth." He preferred champagne, though he said it made him feel as if his foot were asleep.

Looking back at my twenties and thirties, I'm surprised I didn't just throw in the towel, or at least the white linen napkin with which my father swathed his silver wine cradle. By then I was well aware that the world was full of people who didn't like wine, or didn't care about wine, or didn't know anything about wine, or never even thought about wine. Why couldn't I just be one of them?

I wasn't weeping into my milkshakes about it, but neither was I giving up. There were several reasons. One was that I was the *kind* of person who liked wine; therefore, I would like wine. The only question was when. According to my father, civilized minds were naturally drawn to wine. I was civilized! I had swallowed Western culture hook, line, and sinker! I knew the difference between Ben Jonson and Samuel Johnson! More to the point, I knew the difference between Beerenauslese and Trockenbeerenauslese—and even how to spell them! In a column that tipped its hat to my father, the wine critic Robert Balzer wrote, "There are travelers who can cross the great Mojave Desert with no awareness of its awesome beauty, finding it simply arid, monotonous and dusty. There are ears upon which the sounds of Stravinsky or Scriabin fall as strident noise. And there are legions of our fellow countrymen who find the joys of wine much ado about nothing." That wasn't me. It couldn't be, because my father believed there was something actually *wrong* with people who did not love what he loved. He wrote, "When you find a first-rate brain, like Shaw's, rejecting wine, you have probably also found the key to certain weaknesses flawing that first-rate brain." However much I might have liked to deny it, I cared, deeply, what my father thought of me. No way were those certain weaknesses going to flaw a second-rate brain like mine.

Another reason was that I was confident I could learn. Fadimans were big on education. My father had been educated right out of Brooklyn. My mother had been educated right into an appreciation for La Tâche '49. "The childish palate," my father wrote, "will *always* at first prefer the excessive or the unbalanced taste. Upon certain primitive African or Melanesian tribes you cannot confer a greater gift than a can of peaches. That does not make canned peaches a delectable food." Setting aside my suspicion that my father made up this morsel of dubious ethnography, and also setting aside the fact that I didn't like peaches, there was still an encouraging message to be found in the words "at first." If I hadn't been granted the sort of where-have-you-been-all-my-life recognition that had overwhelmed my father when he tasted that white Graves in the Bon Marché department store in 1927, well, then, I could *learn* oenophilia, just as he'd learned how to speak proper English and wear a dinner jacket.

Had he not observed that hosts should serve the best wines they could, even to as-yet-unenlightened guests, because "the palate is as educable as the mind or the body"? My tongue could already speak the language of wine; surely the appetite would follow.

A third reason is that if I liked wine, it would have made my father really, really happy. Jono liked wine; Kim didn't. He still held out hope for me.

So I continued to hope too. And I continued to fudge. When my father flew to New York for his Book-of-the-Month Club meetings, he always took me out to an expensive restaurant, and he always ordered wine. Although I never said I loved it, I never said I didn't. My friends all assumed I did. In my mid-twenties, once I had a regular paycheck from a magazine job, I could be counted on to show up for dinner at their apartments with a dull, safe, mid-priced bottle in hand, always French, usually red (it seemed more sophisticated): Saint-Émilion, Côtes du Rhône, Brouilly. If it was late autumn, a Beaujolais Nouveau.

When I got married, in my thirties, I was grateful to my father for ordering the wines for our wedding. (George is a beer drinker who wouldn't have known where to start.) The red was a Monterey Vineyard Pinot Noir, the white a Julius Kayser Piesporter Michelsberg: budget choices. I think it was beginning to dawn on him that it would be a waste to uncork any Latours for me.

I was even more grateful after Kim opened the borrowed ice cream maker in which he planned to crank five quarts of mint chip ice cream, a festal offering that, to my still-childish but potentially educable palate, no hundred-dollar wine could equal. The canister was rusty. Before you could say "butterfat," my father flagged a cab to a restaurant-supply store on the Bowery, bought a shiny new one, and saved the day.

15

Drunk

My father often mentioned something he called "the letter Hemingway wrote me when he was drunk." It was written on November 26, 1933, on board the SS *General Metzinger*, en route from Marseille to Mombasa. The writer and the addressee had never met. A month earlier, my father had written a *New Yorker* review of *Winner Take Nothing* in the form of an open letter to Hemingway. Though largely complimentary, the review had taken Hemingway to task for rehashing his old themes of sex and blood instead of plowing new ground. It ended with a wicked parody that used bullfighting terminology to describe a game of Ping-Pong. My father's secretary bet him a hundred dollars that Hemingway would be unable to resist responding. She won the hundred.

Late at night, continuing even after the ship's writing room was supposed to close, Hemingway poured out 1,734 words on Gertrude Stein, Leon Trotsky, unappreciative reviewers, and the *General Metzinger*'s toilets, "which burst up like geysers when the ship rolls, plastering your arse with what you hope is at least your own excrement." He sounded angry at everyone but my father, whose review pleased him so much that he extended the cordial invitation "Will be glad to have you come to lunch when I break Max Eastman's jaw." (Max Eastman was one of the unappreciative reviewers.) In the fourth postscript, which wound up and down and around the margins, he wrote:

> Look, I'm 35, I've had a damned fine life, have had every woman I ever wanted, have bred good kids, have seen everything I believe in royally f----d to hell (for Scribner's sake amen), have been wounded many times, decorated many times, got over all wish for glory or a career before I was 20, have always made a living in all times, staked my friends, written 3 books of stories, 2 novels, a comic book and one fairly exhaustive treatise and every chickenshit prick who writes about my stuff writes with a premature delight and hope that I may be slipping. It's beautiful. But I will stick around and write until I have ruined every one of them, and not go until my time comes. So would not advise you to hedge yet.

My father would never have written this letter. Nothing could have induced him to cross his Maginot Line of Permissible Obscenity by using the terms "fucked to hell" (even with four letters redacted in mock deference to a prudish publisher) or "chickenshit prick," or mentioning getting his arse plastered with excrement—especially when addressing a stranger. Nor would he have talked about being wounded and decorated, since he had lived a life of conspicuous inaction in which his chief physical exertions consisted of lifting pens and pulling corks (though he was proud to claim second-or-third-cousinship with Sidney Franklin, né Frumkin, known as the Brooklyn Bullfighter, a friend of Hemingway's who dispatched a large number of bulls with a double-edged Valencia-steel sword and survived three gorings).

I saw my father drunk only once. That is remarkable, given that he drank wine virtually every night of his adult life. The occasion was a family dinner at a Los Angeles restaurant. He and my mother shared a bottle, as usual, but it was the Negronis that preceded it—usually one, but on that evening two or three—which put him over the edge. I'm sure he would have passed a walk-the-line test, but he slurred his words slightly and mixed up a couple of them. I remember this half a century later because it was so anomalous.

Of course he had gotten drunk in earlier decades, starting with the very first time he tasted alcohol. He was fourteen or so. While visiting his brother Ed, he was left alone one afternoon with unfettered access to the liquor cabinet. The most interesting bottle in the cabinet was a small flagon that looked like an artifact from a Grimm's fairy tale. Its label, in Gothic lettering, read "Kümmel." As he recalled, "There was no one to tell me that an ounce of *kümmel*"—a sweet German liqueur flavored with caraway seeds—"is a better thing than two ounces, and a far better thing than twelve ounces." When Ed returned, his little brother was incoherent but not unhappy.

My father's speakeasy days must have contained their share of benders and hangovers, and well into middle age he conformed to the standards of an era in which, as far as I can tell, everyone drank like an unusually capacious fish: a *merlan*, perhaps. When he was in his fifties, *Holiday* magazine sent him first class on the RMS *Queen Elizabeth* to write a series of articles from England. (Oh, how the lot of the journalist has plummeted since the days of the fathomless expense account!) His first night out, he wrote my mother a letter from the ship that, although impeccably phrased, had every reason to sound like the letter Hemingway wrote from *his* ship. "Finished the champagne," he reported, "had a glass of port at dinner, a sherry before dinner, two cigars and two ales—and feel fine." But the multiplicity of beverages was already atypical. He sounded more like the father I knew by the third night of the voyage, when he wrote that he had shared a Château Lafite '52 (a gift from his editor), and the fourth, when he shared a Clos de Vougeot '53. (He derived particular pleasure from the *Queen Elizabeth*'s galley and cellar because they provided such a cheering counterpoint to railroad cuisine, which in his view had grievously declined; after a particularly unfortunate meal in an East Coast dining car, complete with tenth-rate wine, he commented that the Donner Party had eaten better.)

My father wasn't an alcoholic; not even close. He might well have been if he hadn't inclined so steeply toward wine, a tilt that began in his twenties and became more pronounced with each decade. By the time he was in his seventies and we were dining at the Quilted Giraffe, spirits occupied only a small corner of his drinking life.

In his view, wine was not about getting drunk. Pleasantly jazzed, yes; lit up like the Commonwealth, no. The longer I knew him, the better I understood this. Wine was about conversation.

In 1975, he sat down with an interviewer in Milwaukee and, as she described it, "one of the thin Cuban cigars he obtains through devious channels." He posed a question: If the same four people drank martinis on one night and wine on another, how would their conversations differ? He said he'd be willing to bet that on the night they drank wine, their conversation would be mellower, more tolerant, and less egotistical—in short, more civilized.

Milwaukee was not one of my father's usual literary way stations; he stopped there on a book tour to promote *The Joys of Wine*. I had never seen him happier than he was during the years he spent assembling this eight-pound compendium—as one reader described it, not just a coffee table book but a coffee table—of oenological facts, charts, recipes, pictures, stories, poems, and essays, including some of his own. *Joys* provided an opportunity not only to drink a lot of wine and get paid for it but to collaborate with his old friend Sam Aaron, a man of gusto and brio and mojo (as well as many other estimable attributes that didn't end in *o*), for whose wine-store catalogs he had written many introductions over the decades and been paid in many fine bottles. My father called Sam "the vintner of my discontent," but he was precisely the opposite. Fadiman and Aaron went together, according to *The New York Times*, "like Mouton and Rothschild or Moët and Chandon." (The pair was actually a trio. Much of the research was done by John Laird, the nascent connoisseur at my brother's birthday party, for whom a stint on the sales floor of Sam's shop, Sherry-Lehmann, had served as the first rung of his ascent up the wine-industry ladder.)

My father wrote in *The Joys of Wine*, "Generally speaking, we demand something from hard liquor: a punctual reaction. But we expect a wine of quality to demand something from *us*." He pointed out that the Founding Fathers drank wine, and that Andrew Jackson's

Sam Aaron and my father on tour with their oversized offspring, 1975

preference for corn liquor reflected a coarsening of the national tone. To his Milwaukee interlocutor, he observed that our country had two drinking traditions—rum, whiskey, and gin on the one hand, and Prohibition on the other—and that he disliked them equally. Wine was superior to both: "in moderation, of course."

And—though it seems strange to say this about a man who put away half a bottle nearly every night—he *was* moderate. He drank only with dinner. Unlike Hemingway, who said he never drank when he wrote but didn't always mean it, my father would never have drunk wine or anything else while he was working, any more than Julia Child would have drunk while she was on camera. (That glass she raised every time she said "*Bon appétit!*" contained water tinted with Gravy Master.)

16

High

After drinking too much wine with Peter in the New Hampshire farmhouse when I was eighteen, I got mildly muddled on a few occasions, but never more than mildly, which means that—improbably, embarrassingly, pathetically—I have been truly drunk only twice in my life.

In my twenties and thirties, feeling the need for corrupting influences of *some* sort, I dipped a fraction of a toe into a few alternative reservoirs. I bought a small blue glass bong, not because I was a bona fide stoner but because my throat rasped whenever I inhaled an unmediated joint, much as I imagined my father's throat must have rasped when he was breaking in pipes for the rich boys at Columbia. After half an hour, my sense of mild euphoria was trumped by a craving not for the traditional post-smoke extra-large pizza but for a Vicks mentholated throat lozenge. Even after its mollifying passage through my bong's water-filled belly, the marijuana had *too much taste*. Just like wine.

A friend who crashed for a few weeks at my place left a tiny pile of cocaine as a house present. I didn't like it either. Snorting it through a rolled dollar bill made me feel like an idiot and also as if I'd just drunk ten cups of coffee. Why not just drink coffee, which I actually liked? *One* cup, not ten. Consumed through the mouth, not the nose.

The only drug I enjoyed was Ecstasy. I once swallowed two thirds of a 100-milligram tab, painstakingly razored because I figured I weighed two thirds as much as the average male. (I was careful even when I was being careless.) My connection was a friend who had been given a couple of free samples by a psychiatrist he was photographing for *Life*. Ecstasy was still legal when he did the story, but by the time we tried it, it had been reclassified as a Schedule I narcotic: a thrilling transgression for someone so law-abiding that she thought long and hard before jaywalking. Forty-five minutes after I took it, I was sure I would never be grumpy again and uncertain why anyone in the history of the world had ever been grumpy. But during the next couple of weeks, I had an intermittent sensation of warmth on one of my knees, as if a shaft of sunlight were grazing it. Had the Ecstasy messed with my synapses, in which case might the next step be the inability to distinguish between "that" and "which"? And even if I decided to take that appalling risk, could I really imagine myself sallying forth to Washington Square and marching up to a dealer in my little black wool coat buttoned up to my chin and my fuzzy white Icelandic hat, the one that made me look like a mushroom, and saying, "Um, excuse me, sir . . . ," and returning home with a Baggie (was Ecstasy sold in Baggies?) of round white pills that (just my luck) would surely be adulterated with rat poison?

If I wasn't going to take drugs, and I didn't like hard liquor, and I didn't like beer, I was, *ipsis factis*, condemned to a life of monkish sobriety until my wine palate kicked in. *Come on*, I told it. *What are we waiting for?*

The problem was that I sometimes wondered if, despite my ability to roll my *r*s, I might actually *not* be the kind of person who liked wine. Maybe I wasn't educable after all. Even if I drank it in moderation—a foregone conclusion, since even a glass or two left me hot and groggy—I knew I couldn't enjoy wine unless I thought it was fun to get at least a *little* buzzed.

My father certainly did. He wasn't talking about tannins when he wrote, "Neither wine nor hard liquor would be drunk unless they produced effects more interesting than those of milk." Those effects were interesting not only because they were pleasant but also because they granted him a temporary release every evening from the anxiety that had filled his head or lurked in the wings all day: the conviction that he was awkward, counterfeit, permanently stuck in Brooklyn. He found other modes of self-emancipation enjoyable as well. When I was in high school, I discovered a neatly rolled joint in his desk, presumably furnished by the groovy writer with whom he occasionally took walks. My father didn't need a bong.

Release held little appeal for me. The simple truth

was that I was scared of getting drunk. I didn't want to be like Hemingway (indiscretions), or Peter (vomiting), or Charles Lamb (dead log), or Hartley Coleridge (ditches). I had understood my character all too well in the sixth grade when I aligned myself with let's-go-to-the-library Apollo rather than party-animal Dionysus. All my life people had told me to relax. I didn't *like* relaxing. I always took showers, never baths. I hated dancing. I held the steering wheel with both hands instead of draping one arm casually out the window on warm summer days.

William James wrote, "Sobriety diminishes, discriminates, and says no; drunkenness expands, unites, and says yes." Maybe I was just the kind of person who says no.

17

Vintage

I keep in my study an empty Madeira bottle that my father gave me. It has followed me since my twenties, from apartment to loft to house, a reliquary in which reposes not a saint's bones but my father's oenological residuum—his lees, you might say. A photograph I took of it is the wallpaper on my computer, which sits on my desk, ten feet from the bottle. It's a little like looking at a framed picture of your baby while she's sleeping right next to you.

I'm looking at it now: the bottle, not the photograph. It's stubby and wide, like an apothecary bottle, with a cylindrical stopper that was once sealed with wax. Inside, clinging to the clear glass, there is a tobacco-colored pattern of sediment—the desiccated remains of grape skins and pulp—that looks like a map of an imaginary continent drawn by a child.

The liquid that once filled this bottle was made in 1835 on the Portuguese island of Madeira, off the northwest coast of Africa. Madeira was the most popular wine in

My Madeira bottle

colonial America. When my father wrote that the Founding Fathers drank wine, it was Madeira he was thinking of. They used it to toast the signing of the Declaration of Independence. Benjamin Franklin wrote that he would like to be embalmed in a cask of Madeira with a few friends and revived a century later so he could see how his country had turned out.

What I think of as *my* Madeira was shipped in a barrel by John Howard March, a wine trader who also served more than four decades as the island's U.S. consul. The label called it "HOPE" MADEIRA, referring to the ship in which, during the same year that Charles Darwin

sailed to the Galapagos Islands on the *Beagle*, it sailed
to America by a deliberately roundabout route—N. Y.
VIA EAST INDIES—because it was believed that a long,
hot passage, coupled with the rocking motion of the ship,
ripened and mellowed the wine. Well-traveled Madeiras
commanded much higher prices than Madeiras that had
matured on their home island and then hightailed it
across the Atlantic. The *Hope* carried my Madeira across
the equator twice. After it was transferred from barrel to
demijohn to bottle, it ended up, as the label proudly at-
tests, in the cellar of Elbridge T. Gerry, Jr., the son of the
Massachusetts statesman who left one of the smallest
and most unassuming signatures on the Declaration of
Independence. Gerry never drank it, but more than a
century later, my father did.

He could have waited. In 1950, Winston Churchill
drank a 158-year-old Madeira that had once belonged to
Napoleon Bonaparte. As he poured it, he asked the as-
sembled guests, "Do you realize that when this wine was
vintaged, Marie Antoinette was still alive?" Madeira is
one of the longest-lasting of all wines. Like the 1840 port
(*sans nom*) served at my brother's birthday party, it is
fortified with brandy before it has finished fermenting.
The high-proof jolt kills the yeast that would otherwise
continue transmuting the grape sugar into alcohol. High
temperatures—whether on shipboard, in casks stored
in sun-warmed rooms, or in hot vats—contribute to its
mettle, as does deliberate oxidation. The result is stabil-
ity bordering on immortality. Madeira doesn't have to
cool its heels in a thick-walled cellar, nor does it have

to recline on its side, lest oxygen sneak in through a dried-out cork and turn it to vinegar. The sediment pattern of my bottle shows it was stored upright. Heat, air, time: Madeira serenely weathers them all.

My father wrote that wine is "not dead matter, like a motorcar, but a live thing." It moves through the same life cycle as a human being: infancy, youth, prime, old age, senescence. Unfortified wines have shorter life spans than Madeira, but a great red wine, properly stored, can last a century, evolving with each passing decade. It's not like a bottle of Coca-Cola or vodka, exactly the same no matter when you open it. The aging process begins in the barrel, in the presence of oxygen, and continues in the bottle, in its absence—or near-absence, since infinitesimal amounts of air penetrate the cork. The wines that last the longest are those with the most acid and the most tannin, a natural preservative that comes from grape skins, seeds, and stems and is responsible for the astringent quality that made Art Buchwald's mouth pucker when he sampled Château Latour. With the exception of sweet dessert wines, white wines are less durable because the tannin-rich grape skins are removed from the juice before fermentation—which is also why they're white, since the juice of all grapes, both red and white, is nearly colorless; it's the skins that provide the pigment. Most wines made today are meant to be consumed immediately: storage is expensive, attention spans are short. But as a vintage Bordeaux or Burgundy matures, its tannins mellow, its acids soften, its bouquet develops, its character deepens. It ages well.

As did my father. He had started off his career as the

youngest man to hold his multihyphenated jobs; he eventually became the oldest. "I can't retire," he said. "I wouldn't know what to do." Long after his blond pompadour turned gray, he continued to work as a judge for the Book-of-the-Month Club, serve on the board of editors of the *Encyclopædia Britannica*, and assemble anthologies, including a collection of literary and historical anecdotes he described as "appropriate for my anecdotage." In his seventies, he learned child-level Spanish, Italian, Portuguese, Swedish, and Dutch in order to research his long-planned critical history of children's literature, the one for which, decades earlier, he had interviewed P. L. Travers while I poured tea from the set that had once belonged to an earl. Despite his fondness for radio and his distaste, as he put it, for "reacting, like a conditioned animal, to a teleprompter and a little red light," he delivered weekly commentaries for a PBS book series. He still worked at his eighteen-square-foot steel desk seven days a week, as he had throughout my childhood, but taking off Christmas morning to open presents no longer seemed so difficult. His tannins were mellowing.

Over his bed he hung—or, more likely, given his uneasy relationship with hammers, asked my mother to hang—a red-framed excerpt from a thousand-year-old Anglo-Saxon poem called *The Battle of Maldon*:

> *Hige sceal þe heardra*
> *heorte þe cenre*
> *mod sceal þe mare*
> *þe ure mægen lytlað*

The indoorsman outdoors, 1982

He had asked me to copy the lines for him. I obliged, in the same pretentious calligraphy I used on my brother's menu. They meant: "Mind shall be firmer / Heart be keener / Mood shall be more / As our might lessens."

Most of the time he rose to that anonymous poet's challenge. When he was eighty, he told me, "If you are not a nuisance to other people and you are not really sick, all you are is old. Therefore, you don't lift heavy weights, you don't go on ten-mile hikes, and"—he flashed a sardonic grin—"you confine yourself to three or four fornications a day instead of fifteen." But beneath his customary high spirits, which were unfeigned, lay a darker strain, like a somber cello that lurks beneath a chorus of jaunty violins. That cello was not the dominant tone during my father's later years, but there were times when it had been. Once every decade or so, like a comet with an irregular orbital period, depression made an appearance.

The first episode that I know about took place while my father's marriage to Polly was disintegrating. He called this unhappy period "my dark night of the soul" and medicated it, on a winter evening, with what he later remembered as a 1927 Cockburn port. He was alone in his office, the wind was howling outside the window, and after two hours and half the bottle, he felt much improved. "Not that my troubles were forever dispelled," he wrote. "But the wine, in every sense generous, had so illumined my spirit that I could now contemplate those troubles—not with self-pity, but instead with irony and some serenity. As Edmund Spenser says in *The Faerie Queene*: 'Sleep after toil, port after stormy seas.'"

Later bouts of depression were less easily subdued, perhaps because his doctors prescribed antidepressants rather than port. For several months, he would be brought low by sadness, fuzzy concentration, nighttime anxiety, loss of appetite, and baseless worries about money. And then, as if tied to a helium balloon that was just waiting for the right wind, he would rise again, and his essential joie de vivre would prevail for many years, though always with a trace of melancholy under the surface, lending him a measure of gravity not found in completely happy men.

When life was sweet, as it often was, what fun he could be! His exhilaration never had a manic edge; he was simply *merry*, like Fezziwig or Tom Bombadil. He walked around the house singing nonsense songs and chanting macaronic rhymes to whose significance only he held the key. (A favorite was "Corry botkin, corry botkin / Old Professor Plotkin!" We always wondered who Professor Plotkin was. I pictured him with a white beard, a mittel-European accent, and an ear-to-ear smile.) After a tonsillectomy for which I'd returned home from New York, he alternated reading aloud to me from *War and Peace* and talking (or, in my case, passing him notes), and as the puns flew and the air crackled with his real and my pantomimed laughter, I forgot that my throat was too sore to speak. When we went to Europe, he fairly fizzed with excitement as he puzzled out newspapers in languages he was learning, taught me handy expressions from Berlitz phrase books (I can still ask for the bathroom and the Lost and Found Bureau in Italian), combed his Temple Fielding guide for regional specialties (*horchata* in Madrid, almond pastry in Pithiviers), and in Paris—his favorite place in the world—took the Métro with me to the last stop on Ligne 3 because he loved *A Sunday on La Grande Jatte* and wanted to stand where Seurat had stood. On a Florida vacation when he was eighty-three, we rented bicycles; I was afraid he'd crash, but he threw his leg over the saddle for the first time in three or four decades and, with an expression first of intent concentration and then of pure glee, teetered off down the driveway of our rented condo. The topmost rung of his hedonistic hierarchy was occupied by food, wine, and the activities that surrounded them: painstakingly arranging the cheese and pâté on a brass-handled porcelain tray on the one evening each week he was responsible for "cooking" dinner; opening a menu and spotting something he really

liked—mulligatawny soup, veal goulash, osso buco—
and exclaiming "Hotsy totsy!"; taking the first sip of
the wine he'd chosen and, after a brief pause in which
one could feel the entire world aligning with his aspira-
tions, turning to the waiter and saying, "Thank you.
That's very nice."

During his old age, my father spent a good deal of
time thinking about his early life on both sides of the
river he'd crossed. Part of him still felt tethered to his
family's triple-locked apartments in Brooklyn. Part of
him still belonged to Hartley Hall at Columbia, his dorm
during the semesters he could afford to live on campus,
in which he had stayed up till dawn discussing Plato and
Rilke with A, C, D, E, F, and G. He did not miss Brooklyn; he never spoke nostalgically about the gaslights or
the horse-drawn delivery wagons or the steep basement
stairs he had descended in order to shake the ashes in the
coal-burning furnace. He missed Columbia tremendously,
along with the academic career it had falsely promised.
Neither of those selves belonged to the place he currently
lived: late-twentieth-century America, home of the sit-
com and the ketchup-slathered fast-food burger. He felt
that the world of WASP cultivation he had worked so
hard to master—Western literary canon, smoked salmon
on toast points—had slipped from his fingers and been
replaced by vulgarity and ugliness.

Late in his life, he told Kim that among the many
things he loved in the Galsworthy story "Quality" ("Id is
an Ardt"), the scene he thought about most often was the

one in which the old shoemaker looks sadly at a pair of newfangled boots, bought elsewhere, that a customer has worn to his shop. His finger instinctively finds the spot where the left boot, endeavoring to be fashionable, is a shade too tight, and says quietly, "Id 'urds you dere."

My father frequently spoke of feeling out of place, out of sync, as vestigial as an appendix. Id 'urd him, dere and dere and dere, when he was instructed by waiters to "Enjoy!"; was urged (apropos of his feelings, his money, or the contents of his dinner plate) to "Share!"; bided his time on hold while recorded pop singers caterwauled in his ear; tried to write on hotel desks whose surfaces were covered with magazines, video guides, health-club notices, and leatherette-bound directories to services he didn't want; found himself unable to understand young movie actors who omitted consonants and swallowed one word out of three; witnessed the debasement of the English language, both written and spoken. When he heard someone on television employ correct grammar and enunciation—William F. Buckley, for instance—he said the speaker stood out from the multitude "like a baboon with a blue behind." He made lists of words and phrases he particularly disliked, many of them with roots in business or advertising: viable, parameters, timeframe, feedback, breakthrough, target area, quality time, in-depth, cutting-edge, counter-productive, in terms of, in the context of, crispy, crunchy, zesty, have a good one, there you go, you better believe it. "I am quite convinced," he wrote, "that should I live to be 120, I would be unable to understand 90% of what I would hear, unless I spent my life attending meetings of the Modern Language Association. This bleak prospect has its silver lining. It helps reconcile me to death. This is not a joke." He worried that America was descending into a phase similar to the Dark Ages, in which humanism would be replaced by technology. Computers had encouraged people to think like machines, reducing human interactions to "problems" in need of "solutions"—hence the rise of "No problem" (instead of "Certainly, sir") as a catchphrase used in situations, such as reserving a restaurant table, in which no problem could possibly exist.

He reported two related, recurrent sensations. The first was that his outer life (events, career, achievements) felt like a dream, whereas his inner life (thoughts, intuitions, emotions) felt more real every day. This wasn't a metaphor; he told me the experience was as concrete as putting a hand on a hot stove. The second was that his seven-year-old self felt like *him*, whereas the man he had become over the intervening decades felt like an impostor.

He described these feelings in his journal:

Many small children, naturally enough, are socially shy. Anyone would be, if forced to join a game of whose rules he was ignorant. But I remember that I was unusually shy, awkward, ever on the alert for an alcove of retreat. . . . While at the time (age seven or so) I did not understand this, the fact was that there were only two ways to go: retreat even further or compensate.

He chose compensation, became an adult, and spent fifty or sixty years working successfully in the public eye. "The shy seven-year-old was repressed," he continued,

> while I engaged in "experience," an elaborate process of faking it. Now, in my dotage, he has re-emerged, fundamentally unchanged. I am again shy, awkward, retreating. . . . It is as if the imminence of the final fact of death has made it possible for me to rid myself of the Impostor Syndrome. Some force, quite incomprehensible, is quietly divesting me of my costume, acquired or manufactured over more than a half-century, leaving me both naked and free.

A man who is naked and free has no reason to conceal anything and could not do so even if he wished. Our father had always been the more private of our parents, telling Kim and me only about the aspects of his life that made good stories. But as an old man, he was suddenly seized with an almost frenzied need to figure himself out and the urge to transmit his findings to us, whether or not they were entertaining. This was the idea behind *Outside, Looking In*, the book-length essay, intended for his children, that he described in his letter to Dorothy Van Doren. It was also a major theme of the taped conversations we had when I was writing the *Life* story about him: hour after confessional hour about his fears and his failings. Perhaps he felt close enough to death that he could smell his obituaries, which he knew would focus on the successful adult rather than the trembling seven-year-old, and wanted to cut through the bullshit (or horseshit) before it was too late.

He had suffered from insomnia all his life, but the older he became, the worse it got. Sometimes he whiled away the small hours by setting himself word problems, such as naming trees that began with each letter of the alphabet (acacia, baobab, chestnut, dogwood . . .); naming authors beginning with *A* whose names *continued* with each letter of the alphabet (Aanrud, Abelard, Ackerley, Addison, Aeschylus . . .); making up humorous aphorisms ("How pleasing that the Milky Way is both lactic and galactic"); composing clerihews ("Harry Houdini / Sawed a woman in two, the meanie / Leaving neither fraction / Feeling any great satisfaction"); and inventing alternate definitions for common words ("tapioca" should be a Latin-American dance; "Migraine" should be a character in an Arthurian legend).

And sometimes he just lay in the dark, trying to answer the question *Who am I?* Around 3:00 a.m., he'd turn on his bedside light and write in his journal, which is to say he scrawled something on a scrap of paper that would eventually be typed up by his part-time secretary. His journal reminded me of Darwin's "Recollections of the Development of my Mind and Character," written near the end of his life for his children and grandchildren, which skated lightly over the voyage of the *Beagle* but dwelled at length on his essential but not always admirable traits, including gullibility, squeamishness, incapacity for abstract thought, and a tin ear for music. Like Darwin, my father had little interest in recounting his outer life; he was trying, through self-description and reminiscence, to pin himself down. He was neat. He was fussy. He was easily humiliated. He could spot typos from a mile away but was a poor general observer. He viewed objects as enemies. (I once heard him mutter, as he tried to remove his Aquascutum raincoat from an overfull closet, "I hate your guts, Coathanger, and I wish you were dead.") He flustered easily except when he was on the air or on a lecture platform, in which case his desire to call favorable attention to himself trumped his anxiety. He preferred instrumental to vocal music, short poems to long. He was physically clumsy. He was afraid of computers, fax machines, and cigarette lighters—he always lit his cigars with a match—but courageous in matters of honor.

He titled one journal entry "Triumph and Humiliation." He wrote that the memory of dozens of humiliations could be evoked by the slightest of stimuli, but it had taken several nocturnal hours to summon up three memories of authentic triumph. Two of them involved aggression. (This was a trait I never witnessed except when he was watching televised boxing matches, during which he chomped fiercely on a cigar, grunted with every punch, and whenever a particularly good one landed, shouted, "Oh, baby!") When he was ten, a local bully named Beebee falsely accused him of spying on the prettiest girl in their grade. He knocked out two of Beebee's teeth and was carried home on an American flag by a dozen cheering classmates: perhaps the proudest half hour of his life.

Twenty years later, a Fifth Avenue department store

substituted an inferior model for a fur coat his first wife
had taken in for repairs. "The store became another Beebee," he wrote.

> It took only a few minutes to devise a fight plan. I
> snatched up the fur coat, thrust a can of talcum powder
> into my right-hand pants pocket, proceeded to the store,
> contorted my face into a mask of insane rage, frightened
> a salesgirl into leading me to the vice-president's office,
> excoriated him and his associates, and jiggled the hid-
> den talcum can in what I considered the proper gangster
> manner. The bluff worked. Convinced that he was deal-
> ing with a lunatic toting a concealed weapon (he was
> 50% right), he allowed as how the store had made an
> unfortunate mistake. The original purchase, perfectly
> repaired, arrived in good time.

The third triumph came after he received his first paycheck for *Information Please*. He specified that he didn't
feel victorious *when* he received it. "I was happy to get it,
but no more than happy," he wrote. The glory was yet to
come.

> Without hesitation I bolted from my Manhattan apart-
> ment, hailed a taxi (an unheard-of extravagance) and
> was driven to my parents' humble living quarters in
> Brooklyn. The weather was warm, the sun shone. Al-
> most conspiratorially I asked my mother and father to
> come out on the porch, where family conversation was

traditionally set. Dramatic pause for effect. Then, awed by my power, I said, "You will never be poor again."

He confessed to his journal that he was jubilant not because he would be able to make his parents' lives more comfortable but because he had just refuted their long-held assumption that he would never find work when he grew up because all he could do was read.

I believe these three moments of triumph were inextricably bound up with his recurrent feeling that his outer life was merely a dream and his shy, awkward, afraid-to-fight seven-year-old self was the real Clifton Fadiman. He claimed they were his *only* moments of triumph. That sounds absurd, but if they allowed him to transcend that inferior self without feeling like a fraud, it makes sense. You might expect that his successes at Simon & Schuster, *The New Yorker*, and *Information Please*—even the pleasure of *receiving* his first big check—would have counted for more than a couple of knocked-out teeth, a talcum-powder can, and a conversation on a Brooklyn porch. No.

When he was eighty-seven, he selected his favorite journal entries (including "Triumph and Humiliation"), sorted them by theme, and mailed them to his agent. He titled the manuscript *Worth a Jot*. He dedicated it TO SUSANNAH.

Susannah is my elder child, born when my father was eighty-five. By that time, I'd moved up in the world from the apartment with the broken kitchen window to a

SoHo loft, acquired when lofts cost less than expensive cars, in a former box factory whose freight elevator still bore the koan-like sign WE KNOW YOU ARE OLD AND FORGETFUL, BUT PLEASE RETURN THIS ELEVATOR TO THE GLUEING DEPARTMENT. My father ascended in that elevator to pay us a visit whenever he came to New York for a Book-of-the-Month Club meeting. He was an excellent grandfather. In a sense, he'd been prepping for the role for decades, through his research on children's literature, his work as a founder of *Cricket* magazine, and his insistence that small children were "a superior race, possibly Martian invaders who under our influence are gradually assumed to lose the memory of their native land." When Susannah was a baby, George and I were so anxious to keep her happy that we exhausted ourselves by changing our shtick every fifteen seconds: a new song, a new funny face. My father just kept on doing whatever he was doing, slowly and calmly, whether it was drawing from his impressive repertoire of Mother Goose rhymes, alternately tapping his nose and hers with the tip of his finger, or mesmerically chanting her name over and over again like an elderly Jewish swami in a suit from Saks. She stared into his black-rimmed glasses with an intent expression for improbably long stretches, as if she had forgotten that babies cry. A few days before her first birthday, as he crouched before her in an attitude of tranquil expectancy, she took her first steps, straight into his arms. In *Worth a Jot*, he wrote, "I, close to death, am without ambition for myself and, in her way, Susannah has no ambitions for me. We are well-satisfied with each other. Peers."

Worth a Jot was never published. His agent sent it out; it was rejected. I've run the 421 pages through a three-hole punch and put them in a loose-leaf binder, but I wish there were a good-looking hardback, with a photo on the back, to place on my shelves with the rest of my father's books: four collections of essays and criticism, four children's books, four translations, twenty-three anthologies, a high school textbook, a book of anecdotes, and nearly a hundred books to which he wrote forewords or afterwords. The books he wrote himself are all compilations of shorter work; aside from his slim volumes for children, he never wrote what he called "a whole book." He never completed his critical history of children's literature, though the books on which he hoped to base it sat reproachfully in his study for more than two decades; or *Outside, Looking In*; or a cultural critique called *Technobarbarism* he planned to write when he was in his seventies; or a book called *American Novelists and American Life* he planned to write when he was in his thirties; or a novel "about a boy and a girl" he planned to write when he was in his twenties. Why not? It had nothing to do with his work ethic, whose kilowattage could have powered his entire neighborhood. I think that in some way he felt he didn't *deserve* to write a whole book, just as he once turned down a job as editor-in-chief of the *Encyclopædia Britannica* because he felt he didn't deserve it. He felt he deserved to review books, and translate books, and collect other people's work into books, and write short pieces that could be aggregated into books, but not to sit down at his desk, like the authors he reviewed, and watch three hundred pages—which, because he had such high critical standards, would have to be deathless—flow from his fountain pen.

In his fifties, he wrote, "When you reread a classic you do not see more in the book than you did before; you see more in *you* than there was before." In his eighties, there was more in him than there was before. Most people narrow as they age; he broadened. Perhaps his sense that he was regressing to his seven-year-old self enabled him to access a child's openness to new experience. Though he was suspicious of computers, he was also curious, and during a visit in the early days of the Internet, I searched his name on my laptop. His eyes widened when nearly a hundred entries popped up. (Now there are 240,000.) "Remarkable," he said, referring not only to the number but to the Internet itself and my astonishing ability to use it.

His literary tastes expanded. A section of favorite quotations in *Worth a Jot* included plenty of the usual suspects—Montaigne, Henry Adams, Francis Bacon—but also a sentence by June Jordan ("The street set up that way so cars can clip the people easy kill them even") whose grammar and punctuation would once have caused him lasting pain. He collaborated with a specialist in Asian culture on a new edition of *The Lifetime Reading Plan*, a guide, originally written solo nearly forty years earlier, to one hundred books he believed everyone should

PHOTOGRAPH BY MAXWELL COPLAN

CLIFTON FADIMAN: "These authors are life companions. Once part of you, they work in and on and with you until you die. They should not be read in a hurry, any more than friends are made in a hurry. This list is not something to be 'got through.' It is a mine of such richness of assay as to last a lifetime." — from the Introduction.

THE WORLD PUBLISHING COMPANY · CLEVELAND AND NEW YORK

1964

The back cover of the original Lifetime Reading Plan

read over the course of his or her life as "a source of continuous internal growth." The initial list of authors, many of them drawn from John Erskine's General Honors course at Columbia, included only three women—Jane Austen, Emily Brontë, and George Eliot—and not a single non-Western author. The revised list included Lady Murasaki, Sei Shōnagon, Valmiki, Kālidāsa, Ts'ao Hsüeh-ch'in, Omar Khayyam, R. K. Narayan, Yukio Mishima, and Chinua Achebe, among many other interlopers who would undoubtedly have caused Professor Erskine to raise an eyebrow.

When my father was eighty-seven, he flew to New York to have surgery for spinal stenosis. I'd chosen a distinguished neurosurgeon at Mount Sinai Hospital, whose Jewishness mildly annoyed him—were there no doctors at Columbia Presbyterian?—but into whose custody he grudgingly remitted himself. I hired a private nurse to take care of him there for several days after his operation. Of course, because he was an insomniac, he couldn't sleep. He was damned if he wasn't going to get his money's worth, and damned if he wasn't going to find a point of intellectual commonality. Where did the nurse live? Harlem. Was she by any chance familiar with the Harlem Renaissance? Of course she was. What about Langston Hughes? One of her favorites, as well as number 36 on the "Going Further" list at the end of *The New Lifetime Reading Plan*, a sort of honorary purgatory for authors who might someday join the canon. And so, between 2:00 and 4:00 a.m., a light glowed in an eighth-floor room above 101st and Madison while two tired people discussed "Dream Deferred," "April Rain Song," and "Madam and the Rent Man."

My father had long associated books and wine: they both sparked conversation, they were both a lifetime project, they were both pleasurable to shelve, they were the only things he collected. *The Joys of Wine* called wine cellars "wine libraries." As his taste in books broadened, so did his taste in wine. "Brief History of a Love Affair," written when he was fifty-three, mentioned thirteen French and five German wines. That was it for Europe. North America was represented by a single vineyard in New York State. In his late sixties, after he and my mother moved from Los Angeles to Santa Barbara—closer to wine country—he started exploring California wines with, as he put it, "an open mind and a catholic palate." At seventy, he wrote, "What a charitable provision of God or physiology to design our palates so that they remain, one hopes to the very end, not only educable but eager for education." By his mid-eighties, his wine cellar, which had previously been an exclusive French club with an occasional German or Italian admitted on sufferance (but only if he was very well behaved), had become a multicultural potluck. Greece! Chile! Australia! Corsica! Yugoslavia! Everyone's welcome! Come on in! Take off your coats!

His democratic enthusiasm was not boundless. "I would have been no less happy had some of the labels and the contents remained unfamiliar," he wrote. That meant he hated them. English good manners, of course, demanded more diplomatic phrasing. "On the other hand,

I am grateful for a dozen new experiences, journeys into hitherto unknown wine worlds, little astonishments, minuscule enhancements of life." One of his most attractive qualities was his ability to change his mind. Half a century earlier, when he was reviewing books for *The New Yorker*, he used to reserve his final column each year for reappraisals of books he had underestimated, overestimated, or ignored on the first go-round. He called it his annual donning of sackcloth and ashes. Many books got a second chance, and so did he. His openness to wines he'd previously written off was another second chance.

On occasion, he even ignored the classic rules of wine pairings. I knew he'd really loosened up the night he drank a German white with a large plate of spaghetti.

18

Birthday

My father had two eightieth birthday parties. Both were thrown by the Book-of-the-Month Club, which had been among his many employers for precisely half his life. During those forty years his fellow judges had come to look forward to his comments on potential BOMC selections. On a book about Mount Everest: "We should take it because it's there." On a memoir by a Jesuit priest: "A hundred pages of virtue is all right, but 750 pages is too much." On a book about bees: "It would be all right if our membership were made up of bees, but we have only a small number of bees—not enough to make any money out of them." On *Catcher in the Rye*, whose greatness he recognized months before it was published: "That rare miracle of fiction has again come to pass: a human being has been created out of ink, paper, and the imagination." Forty-six years later, J. D. Salinger joined Langston Hughes in the list of classics-in-waiting at the end of *The New Lifetime Reading Plan*.

Bow-tie assistance before his eightieth birthday party, 1984

Celebrating later with Jono, who likes champagne, and Kim, who doesn't

The first party was a black-tie dinner for sixty at the Four Seasons, a New York restaurant, known for its Carrara marble pool and its Picasso tapestry, that was even more famous than La Pyramide, though its cognoscenti may have been more cognizant of money than of gastronomy. My father was in an excellent mood because earlier that day, after he called room service at the Hotel Intercontinental and ordered a ham sandwich without garnishes, a very large white plate had been delivered with two small naked triangles in the center: no lettuce, no tomato, no pickle, no potato chips. "That's the most beautiful sandwich I ever saw," he said in an awed voice. "I've been waiting eighty years for this." A few hours later, when my mother knotted his bow tie from the front, he cheerfully observed, "That's how morticians do it."

This time I did not calligraph the menu. It was printed on a facsimile of the front page of *The New York Times* from May 15, 1904, the day of my father's birth. The headlines included CHINESE RISING AGAINST RUSSIANS, HOLY WAR PREACHED IN TIBET, and CLIFTON FADIMAN BORN: BROOKLYN STUNNED BY GREAT EVENT. That last story, a collaboration between Sam Aaron and me, had been inserted into the two left-hand columns. Among its scoops: "Fadiman's mother, Grace, was heard to complain that her son had turned down a bottle of milk and asked instead for a bottle of Château Mouton Rothschild '29. His father, Isadore, explained that this request would be difficult to fill because it was only 1904."

The center of the page listed the six courses and their

accompanying wines—or perhaps I should say the five wines and their accompanying foods. The wines were chosen by Sam. One of them—Boyer Brut, a quasi-champagne akin to the Brut Crémant on which I got tanked at fifteen with Monsieur Cosnard des Closets—was described on the menu as "Cuvée Fadiman" (Special Batch Fadiman) and merits a bit of exegesis. By some feat of legerdemain, Sam had arranged to have the real label on every bottle replaced with one that bore my father's photograph, flanked by bunches of grapes. On the left, the label read: "Won Gold Award as best French Sparkling Wine produced in the 1981 Vintage." On the right, it read: "Won Double Gold Award as best human being produced in the 1904 Vintage."

Three weeks later, the Book-of-the-Month Club hosted a smaller but in some ways even more memorable celebration at its monthly luncheon meeting. As usual, my father sat at the head of the table. As usual, there was good food and wine. Not as usual, the wine included a Château Lafite Rothschild 1904. It was a gift from Sam. He had chosen nothing less than the most famous wine in the world, a *Premier Cru* Bordeaux from a property on which vines had grown since 1234, a liquid "comparable to the ambrosia of the gods of Olympus" (according to the Duc de Richelieu, who credited to its frequent consumption the sexual vigor he maintained until his death at ninety-two).

My father and the wine were exactly the same age. I know the bottle well because he gave it to me. I keep it in my study, next to the 1835 Madeira: a wine library of

An 80 Gun Salute to
CLIFTON FADIMAN

THE WINES	THE MENU
Boyer Brut Blancs de Blanc 1981 Cuvee Fadiman	Savories
***	***
Trefethen Cardonnay, 1981 (Napa Valley)	Medaillon of Salmon with two Caviars
***	***
Vieux Chateau Certan 1976 (Pomerol)	Filet of Veal Four Seasons Spring Vegetables
***	***
1952 Vintage Port, Ferriera (Portugal)	Two Cheeses
***	***
	Lemon Sherbet with Poached Pineapple and Strawberries
	***
Armagnac 1960 Vintage Private Reserve DeMontal	Mignardises Demi-Tasse
***	***
Four Seasons May 9, 1984	Maitre d' Oreste Carnevali
Menu conceived in 1904 Executed in 1984	Chefs de Cuisine Seppi Renggli Christian Albin Bruno Comin

The eightieth-birthday menu at the Four Seasons

two, though without the wine, displayed on a shelf above a large library of books. The scene on the label is as layered as a Japanese landscape painting: a grand château in the background, with two towers, one conical and one shaped like a pepper pot; then a wide terrace; then a line of trees; then a slender pond; then two laborers wielding rakes; then two gentlewomen in voluminous skirts, serenely taking it all in.

The bottle was shown to the table, but its contents had wisely been decanted. An octogenarian *Premier Cru* Bordeaux could be forgiven for throwing a little sediment.

My father said, "I don't think we'll get much of a bouquet." He stuck his nose cautiously into his glass.

He raised his head. "I think it won't have *gone*, but it may have gone lifeless," he said. His voice grew reflective, a signal that he was entering storytelling mode. "I was once invited to a wine tasting with seven or eight people at Gene Tunney's. He'd recently bought the wine cellar of a German baron. Great Moselles from 1899 and 1900. Rheingaus from 1878. We were agog. But they had all gone flat, every one. Every time we took a sip, we looked up at this great prizefighter, six feet one and a half, and said, '*Interesting*.'"

He rolled his glass.

He sipped.

"Interesting, Mr. Tunney?" said Wilfrid Sheed, one of his fellow judges.

"Better than interesting," said my father. "I can't say it's great. But it is quite healthy. Of course, I'd drink as much as possible in any case, just to have it inside me as an historic relic." (Leave it to my father to say "*an* historic relic," not "a historic relic.") "Of course, it's amazing when anything survives to the age of eighty."

My father had once written about Gene Tunney's interesting wines. He described them as "noble ectoplasms." For reasons of discretion—or perhaps because he feared that if he offended Tunney, he might end up with a left jab to the jaw—he transformed the boxer into a nameless football player who "could have demolished any seven of us poor indoor creatures at a blow."

When I drank my allotted inch of Château Lafite Rothschild 1904, I couldn't have said whether it was great, or healthy, or a noble ectoplasm. Of course, I had no idea what it *should* have tasted like. But the name stirred me. It meant something to me, too, to have the wine inside me as an historic relic.

As my father drank his half glass, I looked at him carefully. He had dropped the banter and had a strange expression on his face. He was concentrating hard. His social smile, in which his lips were pursed slightly as if to form the ideal passage for an incipient witticism, had been replaced by the smile of a child, guileless and wide. But he also looked as if he might cry.

A month later, I visited my parents in Santa Barbara. I drank wine with them at dinner every night. My father was pleased that the three of us could get through a whole bottle, since for years he and my mother had been able to manage only a half, and he usually had to recork it and finish the rest the next evening. One night he served us a

'79 Bandol red from Provence. He asked me if I liked it. I said yes.

I was lying. Or hoping. Or a combination of the two.

I'm pretty sure he knew that. He never said he was disappointed, just as he had never said he was hurt when I ditched him at the Father-Daughter Picnic. And I never confessed. It was more like a daughter feeling sure that her kind but conservative father knows she's gay even though she hasn't come out to him. And that makes me sad, because during my father's old age so many other truths were exchanged.

When he was fifty-three, he had written:

> I cannot leave much, but I have carefully seen to it that I own more wine than I can possibly drink before I die. (This is not hard to do; forgo a suit of clothes—no man needs to buy more than one every five years or so—and you have the wherewithal for three cases.) What good will three thousand dull dollars, which can at best yield five or six percent, do my son as compared with a thousand inherited bottles of wine, guaranteed to generate cheer and laughter and good talk long after my last swallow?

He said "son," not "daughter"—no surprise—but the message was clear. Aside from the minor drawback of having to die first, few prospects gave him more pleasure than leaving behind a legacy of wine.

When he was seventy, the climate had shifted. He wrote:

I am changing my mind about leaving wine to my heirs and assigns. I have come across an acrid injunction by the Roman poet Martial: "Never think of leaving perfume or wines to your heir. Administer these yourself and let him have the money!" I have no opinion about perfume, but Martial may be right about wine. Besides, as the Internal Revenue Service conveniently sees to it that most of us can leave very little cash in any case, I might as well make a clean sweep, do my best to enjoy what bottles remain, and let the next generation enjoy the satisfaction of starting its own collection.

I think he was whistling in the dark when he wrote that line about the next generation starting its own collection. Jono, maybe. Kim and me—well, a midlife conversion was always possible, but the odds were diminishing every year.

By the time he was eighty, he had affixed little handwritten price tags on his most valuable bottles, after consultation with Sam Aaron, so we wouldn't get rooked if we sold them after he died. Although he rarely talked about money outside the family (English good manners), inside the family a different set of rules applied. His letters frequently contained news of profitable book deals and favorable tax refunds, with dollar amounts specified, and were often folded around checks that marked birthdays, augmented my children's educational funds, defrayed the cost of my visits, or reimbursed me for ten-dollar bills I'd slipped him when he took me to dinner in New York and had nothing small enough for the tip.

"Please don't object," he'd write, or "I suggest you use the enclosed as a down payment on the purchase of a new, mentally competent father." A check that was not instantly deposited occasioned a second letter, more pointed in tone, inquiring whether it had "gone astray." He tallied every uptick and downtick of his stocks on green-ruled 11-by-24-inch spreadsheets (I always felt this was like trying to tell time by watching the second hand) and, at year's end, made an annual chart of his "Net Worth," as if his value could be assessed in dollars. When an interviewer asked him to sum up his life in as few words as possible, he responded with four: "He paid his bills." He was proud to have made so much money. He was proud to be generous. He was proud to be able to afford wines expensive enough to warrant appraisal, as if they were gems.

He showed me the bottles with the price tags on that visit to Santa Barbara. They may have been gratifyingly tangible evidence of his wealth, but he felt no pressing need to put them up at the Ritz. A man who does not permit a lettuce leaf to share a plate with a ham sandwich is unlikely to purchase a vibration-free, redwood-lined vault with temperature and humidity controls. The Santa Barbara house, unlike its predecessors in Connecticut and Los Angeles, had neither basement nor pantry, so my father stored his wine in a closet next to the downstairs bathroom, distinguishable from the broom closet only by rows of horizontal shelves to keep the corks moist and holes drilled in the door to ward off mustiness. He had entered his oenologically ecumenical phase: there were wines from France, Germany, Italy, Greece, and California—reds and whites, a few fortified wines, a few dessert wines, some ordinary, some extraordinary. One bottle was labeled "1907 Madeira, $100–$150." Three bottles were labeled "Yquem '37—Sell After My Death, $1000."

"You can sell them to collectors and make a little more," he told me, waving toward the Yquems. His voice was slightly muffled because he was smoking a panatela. "That will take some trouble, though. If you sell them to one of the retail stores here, they'll take them off your hands in ten minutes, sign the check, and you'll be finished."

He told me that his best wines would be worth more with each passing year and that after our mother died, Kim and I might wish to consult someone in order to update their values. "But Sam will be dead," he said. "Everyone will be dead."

He sounded bleak and final, as if he were closing up a long-beloved shop. Then, suddenly, his voice changed. "Well," he said slowly. "I suppose I may still buy a few bottles. Your mother once had a Clos de Bèze '49 that she really liked." He sounded dreamy. "That's a great wine. It was very expensive back then. Fifteen dollars. I suppose it's a hundred now. For her birthday, maybe I'll get a bottle."

19

VIP

I can easily picture my father at ninety. There he is, smiling beatifically, wearing a short-sleeved blue checked shirt he has owned for at least twenty years, his eyes bracketed by laugh wrinkles, his eyebrows still unruly, a respectable fraction of his old pompadour still extant (though now white as milk), sitting at a large desk, but not *the* large desk, since he and my mother have resettled in Captiva, Florida, and because it weighed more than a refrigerator, my mother regretfully decreed that it had to be left behind. The new desk is made of wood and laminate, and its area is considerably less than eighteen square feet, but, like its predecessor, it supports a Scotch tape dispenser and a box of Kleenex and an Indian brass receptacle full of pens and three precisely squared piles of manila folders. In its center drawer there is an envelope labeled "This envelope contains small screw for eyeglasses in case of loss of one."

Captiva was the site of the king's crown conch

expeditions of my youth. In the late 1950s, when we lived in Connecticut, we spent a week on the neighboring island, Sanibel, each spring. Kim and I would look forward all year to the overnight train trip from Penn Station, with its perennial debate over which was superior, the upper bunk (novelty) or the lower bunk (window-shade control), and the rented cottage on stilts, perched on an endless beach, on whose porch railings we displayed our daily gleanings: prickly cockles, apple murexes, lettered olives, alphabet cones, lightning whelks. Thirty years later, when Santa Barbara started to get too crowded and too fashionable, my parents moved to Captiva because the islands had been the locus of our greatest family happiness. George and I visited frequently, and our children collected shells and learned their names and displayed them on porch railings, just as Kim and I had. Susannah had been joined by Henry Clifton Fadiman Colt. George's father was named Henry Colt. We liked to say that his father had swallowed my father.

It all felt like an Indian summer, an unexpected warmth before the expected cold. I'd first noticed the phrase "As I near the end . . ." in one of my father's letters when he was seventy-two. By the time he was eighty, he made death sound only minutes away. He proved an un-reliable forecaster. His old age had lasted for nearly as long as I could remember, but his old old age lasted even longer.

My father's longevity was particularly surprising be-cause, over the course of his long life, he seemed to have suffered nearly every natural shock to which flesh could possibly be heir. He enjoyed boasting about his infirmities. "People talk about radiating good health, as if they were steam furnaces," he once said to me. "What a vulgar thing." In my file cabinets there is a thick folder with a label neatly typed by his secretary: MEDICAL HISTORY, CF—GENERAL. I own it, I suppose, since I am my father's literary executor and therefore inherited all his files, but nothing in this folder is literary. It contains four decades of unpleasant diagnoses: diabetes, arthritis, bursitis, tendinitis, rheumatism, fibromyalgia, degenerative lumbar disc disease, spinal stenosis, atrioventricular block, thyroid imbalance, dysesthesia of the left hand, insomnia, prolapsed hemorrhoids, poison ivy, and flat feet. Also colon cancer, whose only lasting aftereffect, following the removal of a significant fraction of his large intestine a few months before he moved to Florida, was the relief of half a century of constipation. He asked Kim to drive him on a tour of the pharmacies of Santa Barbara so he could attempt to return several giant bottles of Senokot, acquired over the years, of which he would no longer have need and was delighted to be rid, especially if he could get a refund.

When I first opened that folder, I asked myself—as I have asked myself from time to time when looking through the rest of his files in the course of writing this book— *What am I doing here?* Is it appropriate for a daughter to read about her father's hemorrhoids? And what about the photographs he unaccountably kept from his numerous colonoscopies, unseemly pink landscapes that look as if they should never be exposed to light, let alone a daughter's gaze?

Somehow, he survived all these afflictions. Perhaps it was the thousands of gallons of claret and Burgundy he consumed over the years, packed with resveratrol, a phenolic compound in red wine that has been shown to extend the life span of yeast, and possibly of human beings. Perhaps it was just good DNA. His father, Isadore, lived to ninety, though he decided that sounded unbecomingly old and claimed to be eighty-eight for three years.

Relationships with parents wax and wane, following their own natural cycles. I was fortunate to have loved both my parents, and been loved by both, but I sometimes felt closer to one and sometimes to the other. In college, when I was studying English literature, I felt closer to my father. In my twenties and thirties, when I was working as a reporter, I felt closer to my mother. In my early forties, when I started to write essays, the tide turned back in my father's direction. Essays were *his* territory, and I might never have ventured over the border if I hadn't been confined to bed during eight months of Henry's gestation and obliged to find a literary genre that could be executed from a horizontal position. But something else had changed too. There comes a point when oaklings outgrow the diminutive and stop worrying about withering beneath the shadow of the oak. I no longer bristled—a slight sigh sufficed—when I was told, "You're following in your father's footsteps" or "You have your father's genes." He had my genes, too. There had been a time when nothing would have pleased me more than to be better known than he was, but as he grew frailer, I started to worry that someday this might actually happen. If my father were forgotten, the balance of my world would shift so disorientingly that I'd lose my footing. I still check periodically to make sure he has more Google entries than I do. Phew.

A few years ago I received a letter—I suspect something similar went out to every writer in America—asking me to donate copies of my books to the Mother of Civilization Library in southern Pakistan. "Honorable Ma'am," it said. "We therefore anxious in collecting resource materials including any books of Honorable Professor Anne Fadiman internationally well-known, an American author, Editor and Teacher and daughter of renowned literary, radio and television personality Sir Clifton Fadiman." Sir Clifton Fadiman! Now you're talking! It was about time my father was elevated to knighthood. I felt like throwing my hat in the air.

All of which explains why writing essays wasn't intimidating. I was no longer competing with my father.

I continued to call him "Daddy," as I had all my life. When I was a teenager, he had correctly guessed that the name might embarrass me and signed one of his letters "Daddy (or 'Dad' or 'Father' if you seem too old for such nursery terms. Hell, call me 'Chuck,' if you want to!)." But the groove was so well-worn that there was no possibility Dad, or Chuck, would ever gain traction. Now that he was very old, I found myself welcoming the pecking order that "Daddy" implied. His life might be on the decline, and mine on the rise, but I wanted him to know that I still looked up to him and that, in some fashion, he could still look down on me.

As parents age and the balance of dependency resettles, relationships often sweeten and simplify. "I seem to be doing pretty well," he wrote me. "I think often of how much you have done for your ancient father. This particular Lear has more sense than the original: I know a Cordelia when I see one. Love, Daddy."

My father wrote that letter at his desk on Captiva when he was eighty-six, on stationery with an address about as far from Brooklyn as it is possible to imagine ("BEACH HOME 13, SOUTH SEAS PLANTATION"), peering through black-rimmed glasses as his fountain pen traced tiny, tightly spaced letters in upward-sloping lines. (His handwriting was as distinctive as a fingerprint. A friend of his once sent an anonymous sample to a handwriting analyst, who reported: "Here we have a genuine intellectual—a creative and original thinker and brilliant scholar. He is somewhat impractical and maybe fussy about small things.") As I picture him four years later, at ninety, sitting at that desk in his blue checked shirt, not much has changed. But wait. Something is missing. Where are his glasses? He has worn a succession of them throughout my life: champagne-colored, gray shading to black, tortoiseshell, and, finally, plain black. Without glasses, his eyes look smaller, more watery, and more vulnerable, but you can also see the laugh wrinkles better.

The small screw will remain in its envelope in his

center desk drawer for the rest of his life, but he will never need it again.

When he was eighty-eight, he woke up one morning with mildly clouded vision. Few things could have been better calculated to annoy him, since to go for a day without indulging what he called his "odd, parochial mania for decoding black squiggles on white paper" was like being asked to go without breathing. He estimated that since the age of four he had read more than twenty-five thousand books, an achievement that placed him, he said, in the same category as a three-legged chicken. He had spent most of his eighty-eighth year skimming a sizable fraction of all fifteen editions of the *Encyclopædia Britannica* published since 1768 in order to compile 669 pages of extracts, on topics from Phlogiston and Bastardy to Psychoanalysis and Relativity, a feat that, according to a reviewer for the *Chicago Tribune*, called for "a super-heroic anthologist, the literary equivalent of Indiana Jones."

Indiana Jones's work required a revolver and a bullwhip; my father's required his eyes—or rather, at this point, his left eye, since a blocked artery had decommissioned the right one when he was eighty-six. I'd heard about that earlier mishap on the phone; he made it sound hardly more troublesome than a stubbed toe, perhaps because binocular vision is less important for reading than for walking around outdoors, something he took pains to avoid even though his house fronted directly on a beach dotted with tourists who had traveled hundreds, and in some cases thousands, of miles to walk on it.

But this time I happened to be on Captiva, with my

family in tow. His local vision center told him he had an inflammation of unknown cause that would clear up soon, but on the second visit, when I pressed the ophthalmologist on the diagnosis, I didn't like the way he wouldn't meet my eyes—or his patient's, not that my father would have noticed, since his vision was worsening every day.

Characters in trashy novels are often said to have "a bad feeling." I have had plenty of sad feelings and hurt feelings, but this is the only time in my life I remember having an unequivocally *bad* feeling about something— the certainty, without any rational evidence, that a catastrophe was drawing near.

I told my father I was taking him to the Bascom Palmer Eye Institute in Miami. My mother wasn't sure this was necessary, but I booked two plane tickets for the next morning. We woke to a wild storm that carried huge breakers high up the beach and bent the palm trees at improbable angles. In the taxi on the way to the Fort Myers airport, we heard on the radio that all flights had been cancelled. I asked the driver if he would drive us to Miami. He looked at me as if I were deranged—Miami was on the other side of Florida—but, after I offered him an exorbitant sum, he agreed. Highway I-75, locally known as Alligator Alley, was flooded; there were few other cars. As the taxi careened down the middle of the road, the waters parted like the Red Sea. My father seemed as unperturbed as if he were sitting in his living room. Of course, he couldn't see a thing. I wasn't sure our driver could either; the windshield was a blur.

We got to the hospital. Someone took a look at my

father's eye in the emergency room and quickly picked up the phone. By an implausible stroke of luck, one of the world's best-known experts on my father's condition happened to be working in her lab at Bascom Palmer. She arrived at a trot. After examining him briefly with an ophthalmoscope and a handheld lens, she explained that he had acute retinal necrosis, the death of living cells in the retina; that it was caused by the reactivation of a chicken-pox virus that had been latent in his body for eighty years or more; that much of his retinal tissue had already been destroyed; that he would never regain normal sight; that he would be put on intravenous acyclovir to kill the virus; and that in order to try to prevent complete retinal detachment she would attempt to tack down what remained—a fragile, moth-eaten membrane, part viable, part necrotic—with a laser, immediately. Which she did. It was only after she finished that I realized no one had gotten around to asking for my father's ID, let alone his insurance card: a sign of a true emergency.

That night, in his hospital room, dinner arrived on a tray with a little card that said "VIP." "They know who you are!" I said. A tiny flicker of pleasure passed across my father's face. Then it occurred to me that VIP might mean "Visually Impaired Person."

I spent the night next to his bed, on a cot. Because the lights were off, we were equally sightless. It was the first time we had ever shared a room. He told me there were two reasons his life was no longer worth living: he would burden my mother, and he couldn't read. He asked if I would help him die.

A few years earlier I had written an article about an elderly couple, members of the Hemlock Society, who had committed suicide, and he assumed I knew something about methods. I gulped and asked him to do his damnedest for six months, at which point we could have this conversation again. I didn't say I would help him then, but I didn't say I wouldn't, which meant that I knew I'd spend those six months in a state of high anxiety.

He agreed.

After a long pause, he asked me if I would telephone two women when I got home and let them know he had lost his sight. One lived in New York, the other in Chicago. That was all he said. But there was something in his voice as it drifted down from the hospital bed. I instantly knew that these were women with whom he had had affairs.

This did not come entirely as a surprise. A few years earlier, when we were talking after dinner in his room at the Hotel Intercontinental in New York, the phone had rung and he had said, "I told you never to call here." I had wondered, but I had never asked, partly because I didn't want to press him on something he hadn't volunteered, partly because I didn't want to know. Although the timing was accidental, he could hardly have planned a more strategic moment for this revelation than the night at the eye hospital. As I lay on my cot, listening in the darkness, I would have accepted anything, pardoned anything. He could have told me he was a murderer. Nothing would have seemed larger than his blindness.

I'm not certain why he chose to let me know. It might have been purely practical: he feared he wouldn't be able to call his lovers—or perhaps former lovers—himself, even when my mother was out of the house, because he couldn't see to dial the phone. Or he thought he'd soon be dead and wanted to tie up loose ends. Or maybe he just felt all bets were off now and all secrets were moot.

A few days later, I called the women. I was surprised that both of them sounded old—but of course they were old! My father was eighty-eight. I had the feeling he had known them for a long time. They were upset by the news and courteous to me. He didn't mention their names again.

I never found out whether my mother knew. And I never doubted that he loved her. In fact, by this time— when their age difference had become significant and she had spent years taking care of him during his many illnesses—I think he loved her more than she loved him, though she didn't stop *enjoying* him. (Once, after he gave a talk at the local library and charmed the entire reading population of Sanibel and Captiva, she told Kim, "That's why I married that man.") He could inscribe one of his books "For My Darling—And Forever" and mean it, and he could betray her, and he could believe these two acts were not mutually exclusive. He was constitutionally in-capable of resisting a conquest, a thumbs-up, an attesta-tion that he was not an outsider or a fraud or irretrievably ugly. I understood, but my disappointment never went away.

It was a long night at Bascom Palmer. He talked about his work and his family. It all sounded ominously like a summing-up. At some point, near dawn, I reminded him that Milton hadn't thrown in the towel after *he* lost his sight. He'd written *Paradise Lost*. And *Paradise Regained*. And *Samson Agonistes*. Sounding a speck less grim, my father chimed in that Milton had also written "that famous sonnet," and then proceeded to recite the first few words of "On His Blindness."

Fragment by fragment, we managed to piece together the sonnet's first three and a half lines ("When I consider how my light is spent / Ere half my days, in this dark world and wide / And that one talent which is death to hide / Lodged with me useless") and two of the last three ("Thousands at his bidding speed / . . . They also serve who only stand and wait"). Milton was asking a question: If I can't see and I can't write, how do I serve God? And answering it: I don't have to *do* anything; forbearance is a form of service.

At the time, and for many years afterward, I construed the eagerness with which my father leapt to the task of reconstructing the poem as evidence of his ineradicable love of literature, and therefore, potentially, of life. And it was. But now I think a couple of other things were going on as well. One was that we were playing an insomniac game—something he'd always done in the dark and could continue to do in the dark—and it had not stopped being fun. The second was that he was wondering if there was an outside chance that, somehow, he might be able to keep on working after all. Milton talked a good game about being a contented bystander, serving God from the sidelines while the sighted multitudes rushed around serving Him through action, but that was nonsense. There was no way he was going to spend the rest of his life standing and waiting. As my father well knew, Milton ended up dragooning various friends and relatives to serve as his amanuenses, including his daughters, who took dictation and complained bitterly about having to read aloud in languages they did not understand. In short, he became a pest, but he adapted. My father didn't give a damn about serving God, or xbyabt, but the poet's example contained something that, an hour or two earlier, he had been unwilling to acknowledge: possibility.

My father was discharged from Bascom Palmer. My mother drove him home. His retina did not detach, and his vision became slightly less cloudy, but he still could not see the E at the top of an eye chart, and was never able to again. To keep up his end of our bargain, he agreed to attend a day program for adults who had recently lost most or all of their sight. And it is at this point, against all probability, that the tragedy turns into a comedy, in both the Hollywood sense (it's not without humor) and the Shakespearean sense (there's a happy ending).

The program was run by the Visually Impaired Persons Center of Southwest Florida: "VIP" again, a term that, like so many euphemisms, tries to turn dross into gold. VIP was located in North Fort Myers, forty miles and three bridges from Captiva; my father went there from 10:00 to 3:00 every Tuesday and Thursday for six weeks. He knew he couldn't get out of it—he had promised to do his damnedest for six months, and he was a man of his word—but he wasn't exactly champing at the bit. Given his lack of enthusiasm for the American cult of Sharing, it would have been hard to find a less appealing prospect than a "group session" run by a charity. The subject was "independent living skills." He hadn't had an abundance of those even when he could see. What was the point of learning how to cook, wash his clothes, and change his sheets in his ninth decade when he had a wife who already did those things for him, and in six months he'd probably be dead anyway?

On the afternoon of his first class, I sat in my New York loft, waiting for him to call, or rather for my mother to dial and hand him the receiver. The phone rang. I expected the worst.

"That may have been the most interesting day of my life," he said.

I assumed he was being ironic.

"Except for the *first* day of my life," he continued, "it was the most novel. There is nothing in my eighty-eight years of experience that prepared me for it."

He told me that the room had been large; he had initially felt disoriented and bewildered. Several of the staff members were visually impaired themselves—one had explained that she had been blinded by a snowball when she was thirteen; another had taken my father's medical history and amazed him by typing it into a computer—and preternaturally cheerful. He had learned several skills: how to identify bills in a wallet (fold each denomination differently); how to distinguish coins (use your fingertip to gauge the size and your fingernail to feel the smooth or ridged periphery); how to open a milk carton (locate the two vertical edges with seams and press up the spout on the opposite side); how to fill a coffee cup (curl your finger over the rim to detect the rising heat); and how to put toothpaste on a toothbrush (squeeze a dab onto your lower lip, from which it is unlikely to fall, and sweep it up with the brush). "The challenges were of the most mundane character," he said, sounding surprised that he had found them so fascinating. He'd always been bad with his hands (that 6th percentile in Lefthanded Finger Dexterity on the Johnson O'Connor test) and had outsourced all manual labor, with the exception of opening wine bottles, to wives, secretaries, and servants. Learning how to fold and pour and squeeze—and having no doubt that he could do so competently—really *was* novel.

He had expected a roomful of uncongenial boors, and what had he found? An ego-boosting conclave of nice old Jewish ladies, many of them originally from New York, who remembered him from *Information Please*. The fact that he couldn't see them, or they him, was immaterial; fifty years earlier, they hadn't seen him on the radio either. The leader had announced, "We have a celebrity with us today—Clifton Fadiman!" And everyone had clapped. At VIP, my father actually *was* a VIP.

Over the next several weeks, his fellow students turned out to be a more effective tonic than antidepressants, maybe even than a 1927 Cockburn port. He was like an aged and somewhat clueless king who descends from his castle in order to mingle with the people, and discovers he actually likes them. Or at least most of them; I regret to say that he described some of them as "the goddamnedest fools." But he also said they had more character than he did. Most of them were widows living on Social Security; one had two metal knees; another had had multiple cardiac bypasses; many were profoundly blind; and yet they never asked why God, in whom they all seemed to believe, had not treated them better. By contrast, my father was wealthy, he had a wife who took care of him, he was in reasonable health, and though he was legally blind, he retained enough residual vision to make out shapes and not bump into furniture. In the suffering department, he was a comparative piker: a realization that immediately made him stop complaining.

He learned how to follow a sighted guide (hold her arm firmly above the elbow and let her walk a half step ahead). He learned how to shave his neck (swallow so the Adam's apple recedes and doesn't get scraped). He learned how to use a National Library Service Talking Book cassette player (from left to right, press the buttons for Stop, Rewind, Play, Fast Forward, and Eject, each embossed with a symbol). After the last of those lessons, he told me, "I am looking forward to Talking Books," and I told George, "He used the phrase 'looking forward'!"

In the third week, after hearing a VIP student say she

wished that she and her classmates could have Mr. Fadiman all to themselves, the leader suggested he lead a seminar called Fadiman's Conversation Class. My father recruited five enthusiastic acolytes—the group soon doubled—and gave them a homework assignment: listen to Larry King's radio talk show. The next day, just as he had guided clerks and stenographers through the Great Books in the 1920s, he led a discussion in his inimitably plummy voice of King's principal topics. He told me, "Your old man is back at his old job."

The climax of the VIP program—an opportunity to apply many of the skills the students had learned—was a visit to a simulated McDonald's that had been set up at a counter on one side of the classroom. Each of them was given money tucked into an envelope that was labeled "WALLET" in giant letters, for the benefit of the partially sighted. The customers lined up, ordered, paid with carefully folded bills, and received their meals (empty bags and empty milk cartons) and their change (invariably wrong, so they'd have to pay attention to the size and texture of the coins). In my father's case, given his taste for *tournedos Rossini* and his distaste for ketchup, it was just as well that the burgers were imaginary. VIP had doubtless chosen McDonald's because it was a restaurant with which every student in the room would be intimately familiar. Every student, that is, but one. My father was familiar only with the *idea* of McDonald's. He had managed to spend decades complaining about American popular culture without actually experiencing any. Finally, his opportunity had arrived! It is true that it came in an unexpected guise—a fast-food restaurant with no fast food, patronized exclusively by customers who couldn't see it—but what man can predict the form in which his enlightenment will present itself?

In the eye hospital, my father had said there were two reasons he wanted to die: he didn't want to burden my mother and he couldn't read. In the weeks that followed the VIP program, he made headway on both fronts.

Reading was the more straightforward of the problems. Although VIP offered a Braille class, he considered himself too old to learn; and, in any case, why try to read with your fingertips when you could read with your ears? His Talking Book player arrived, and he mastered its five buttons. He had been informed that eighty thousand free books on tape were available, from the Bible to pornography, and though he never availed himself of either of those, he ordered hundreds of others, as well as commercial audiobooks. He had two players, one upstairs, one downstairs on his desk, where he continued to spend most of the daylight hours. Listening to a cassette wasn't as good as reading a book—compared with his former pace of eighty pages an hour, it was maddeningly slow, and he couldn't skip the scenery descriptions—but it was better than he'd expected. He told me his favorite part of the day was climbing into bed at midnight, pressing Play (third button from left, embossed circle), and listening to, say, *Phineas Finn* by Anthony Trollope. (He knew it was midnight because I'd bought him a watch that announced the time in a teeny mechanical voice and tolled the hours with a teeny chime.)

With Henry and Susannah on Captiva, wearing his talking watch, 1996

The other problem was thornier. My mother put in his eye drops and lined up his pills behind his breakfast plate. After she laundered his clothes, she filed them in the same spots in his dresser every week and folded— not rolled, since a tight ball would have been harder to dismantle—his socks in conjoined pairs so that even if he wasn't wearing the ones he'd planned, at least they'd match. She dialed his phone. She cut up his meat. She was interrupted every few minutes throughout the day with a question about where something was or what something said or how to do something, each question accompanied by an apology that made it sadder. Sometimes she was cheerful and sometimes resigned; it's easy to cut up someone's meat the first time and less easy the fiftieth. He'd never taken care of her; on the only occasion I could remember her being truly sick, with toxoplasmosis from breaking up a cat fight, she'd driven herself to a hospital in downtown L.A., and, because he didn't know how to cook dinner, he'd driven me to a restaurant in Beverly Hills whose rear wall was constructed from the bottoms of wine bottles—and backed into the wall.

But VIP had helped. My mother didn't have to dispense his toothpaste or button his shirt or do the hundred other independent living skills he'd learned that made him, if not independent, less dependent.

They often "watched" television together at night, sitting companionably on the upstairs sofa; he could follow *60 Minutes* without much difficulty, and when the plot of *Law & Order* hinged on a visual detail—the length of the victim's miniskirt, the make of the suspect's getaway car—she filled him in. Their best times were at restaurants, at which they continued to dine three times a week. They'd stroll confidently into Chadwick's or Portofino or 'Tween Waters, where the waiters all knew them, my father following half a step behind my mother, holding her arm firmly above the elbow. She'd read him the menu; his ears would prick up if the starters included a good soup, which, once he'd sussed out the dimensions of the bowl, was especially easy to negotiate without incident. He had learned how to reach for a glass without spilling it (move hand slowly along surface of table with fingers curled) and how to avoid oversalting (sprinkle in palm first, then on food). The only part of the evening he didn't enjoy was my mother's handling of the bill, which both offended his sense of appropriate gender roles and made him worry, not without justification, that she would leave an outrageously large tip.

When my father left Bascom Palmer, his doctor had told him that over the coming months, his vision had roughly equal chances of staying as it was, worsening, or improving (though he would always be legally blind). It improved—never enough for him to leave the house without benefit of my mother's arm, but enough to allow him to make out a thirty-point headline, though the print, like everything else in his visual field, was hazy and patchy, as if he were looking through Swiss cheese in a dense fog. Glasses would not have helped, because they would have focused images on a retina too damaged to process them. His mood fluctuated according to his basis of comparison: he was screwed compared with normally sighted people but in clover compared with the profoundly blind, a group he had feared he might join. Most of the time he was in clover. From Maxi-Aids, an "adaptive products" catalog of which the Fadimans became devoted customers, I ordered a telephone with Brobdingnagian numbers, and, after sending him samples of various outsized fonts, some serif, some sans serif ("CAN YOU READ THIS? OR THIS? HOW ABOUT THIS?"), I made a list of essential phone numbers, of which the most frequently consulted were those of his favorite restaurants. Now *he* could make the reservations.

Maxi-Aids also supplied my father with pads of paper ruled with thick, widely spaced black lines. Their arrival marked the return of something he had assumed was gone for good: writing. He wrote with a Magic Marker in capital letters ten times the size of his old handwriting. He couldn't always see his work—sometimes he kept on writing after the marker ran dry—but he could see the black lines, and we could usually decode what he'd written between them. He wrote me many lists of article suggestions for the literary quarterly I edited; I thought of them as lineal descendants of the hundred book ideas he'd once written down for Max Schuster. He resumed jotting down his thoughts at 3:00 a.m.

Some of those jots were wordplay:

THE THREE BEARS: FLAUBERT, D'ALEMBERT, CAMEMBERT

MOURNDAY, BLUESDAY, TEARSDAY, CRYDAY, SADDERDAY, AND THE SOBBETH. (FROM A CALENDAR ISSUED BY THE BOOK-OF-LAMENT CLUB)

BETWEEN A WOK AND A HOT PLATE

Some were more serious:

ANOTHER OF MY INSOMNIA GAMES: ANSWER THE QUESTION, WHAT SINGLE EXPERIENCE OF MANKIND'S ENTIRE HISTORY HAS MOST PROFOUNDLY ALTERED HIS PSYCHE? THE TRANSITION TO ERECT POSTURE? THE SHIFT FROM A HUNTING TO A TILLAGE CULTURE? THE ADVENT OF FIRE? STEAM, ELECTRIC

POWER, ATOMIC FISSION? PERHAPS NONE OF
THESE, AS COMPARED WITH THE DECLINE IN
THE BELIEF IN A LIFE AFTER DEATH.

If he thought of something too long to fit on a Maxi-
Aids pad, he waited until he could dictate it to his part-
time secretary. Anne Marcus was far more accommodating
than Milton's daughters, who smile sweetly in paintings
by Delacroix and Fuseli as their father dictates *Paradise
Lost* to them but were actually so resentful that they stole
from him and sold off part of his library. And if my
father's literary efforts weren't exactly *Paradise Lost*,
they were an accurate record of what was on his mind, a
sort of noetic meter-reading. Here are two:

> This morning I had to substitute a new roll of toilet pa-
> per for the exhausted old one. For a short time I found
> myself vainly fumbling with the simple spring mechanisms
> that fit the roll into the hollow right and left spaces. I
> felt frustration, cursed my ineptness, felt ashamed and
> inferior. But—suddenly I succeeded in inserting the roll
> properly. I felt at once a triumphant satisfaction that
> would be denied the sighted person.

And:

> Every blind person becomes a Thoreauvian. "Simplify,
> simplify!" lay at the heart of Thoreau's message to the
> world. For the blind, the message has no moral implica-
> tions. It represents an entire and compulsory way of life.

He cannot afford, because he cannot handle, even the slightest excess or profusion of objects, movements, even social relationships. His salvation lies not in multiplicity, but in simplicity. (Develop with examples.)

"Develop with examples." What a characteristic Clifton Fadiman imperative! He hoped to assemble a short collection of essays on blindness, to be called *When I Consider*: the first three words of Milton's sonnet, which continued to be much on his mind. He never developed this passage with examples, and *When I Consider* joined his stack of unfinished books. But that turned out to be no tragedy. He found other and possibly more essential fish to fry.

The trickiest lines in Milton's sonnet are "And that one talent which is death to hide / Lodged with me useless." As I knew from Miss Carnes's twelfth-grade English class, Milton was referring not only to his literary talent but to the Parable of the Talents in Matthew 25, the story of a harsh master who, before leaving on a journey, entrusts his three servants with silver talents, an ancient unit of currency. The first two double their talents and are rewarded, but the third buries his in the earth, and when his master returns, he is cast out into the darkness. My father had spent his life being one of the first two servants: a money-maker. He was never going to submit meekly to the prospect of being the third.

Six years earlier, he had heard that the Book-of-the-Month Club's board of judges was about to be dissolved or restructured and thought he would be out of a job.

This turned out to be a false alarm—he was not among the judges who were asked to resign—but for several months he was in a swivet. He asked me what I thought he should do. Well, I said, aquiver with youthful ideal-ism, perhaps he could volunteer as a writing teacher in a prison. A look of distaste and incredulity passed across his face. It took me years to realize that the question of whether he would have wished to spend his days Sharing with criminals was the least of it. The real deal-breaker was that *he wouldn't have been paid*.

Which meant that even if he could dictate his thoughts to an amiable secretary, even if he could continue to dine with his wife in expensive restaurants, even if he could change a roll of toilet paper without help, even if he could listen to Trollope all night, he was not going to be satisfied. He wanted to work. (I will remind the reader of my father's age: eighty-eight. Most eighty-eight-year-olds, even those without acute retinal necrosis, are not fret-ting about buried talents. They're *retired*. But to my father, retirement would have felt like being cast out into the darkness.)

And that led back inexorably to the Book-of-the-Month Club. (His Book-of-Lament Club pun was not a reflection of his true feelings. Lamentation was the last word he would have associated with his esteemed employer of forty-nine years.) Vetting eight or ten man-uscripts a month seemed an unlikely job for a blind man. A Miltonic system of live readers wasn't feasible, since he often preferred to read after midnight. But what if the Club took the money it had previously allocated to his monthly trips to New York and spent it on taping the manuscripts?

I wrote a letter suggesting this to my father's boss, who was extremely fond of him, and she immediately assented. Friends helped us scout out-of-work actors with home tape recorders and exemplary enunciation who were willing to work for twelve dollars an hour. My father listened to audition tapes and chose a Juilliard graduate in New York. She ended up reading about half the books; the other half were read by my brother Kim, who had won speech contests in high school and had a mellifluous voice. (Kim also taped the entirety of my first book.) The completed cassettes, their sides marked with inch-high numbers, were FedExed to my father in Captiva, and his assessments, dictated to Anne Marcus, were FedExed back to New York. (The Book-of-the-Month Club's board of judges was eventually disbanded, this time completely, but my father was retained as "Chief Editorial Adviser," and the interstate cassette traffic continued for the rest of his life: proof that not every American corporation has a heart of stone.)

Six months came and went. My father never mentioned the subject of suicide again.

If he hadn't stuck around, he would have missed the opportunity to co-edit a 1,338-page anthology of world poetry. He listened to the poems on tape, developed an unanticipated interest in medieval Persian literature, and reported that if he'd gotten the job ten years earlier, he would have done it less well because he would have paid insufficient attention to the sounds of the words.

He also would have missed receiving the National Book Award for Distinguished Contribution to American Letters, a prize that had previously been won by Saul Bellow and Eudora Welty, among others. Getting to New York was a logistical feat, but, gripping my mother's arm firmly above the elbow, he managed. At the awards dinner at the Plaza Hotel, he enjoyed the roast rack of lamb; the Robert Mondavi Cabernet Sauvignon; the conversation with Stephen King, who asked me to bring him to our table and gushed as sweetly as a teenage fan; and the envelope that contained the ten-thousand-dollar check. In his acceptance speech—delivered, of course, without notes—he developed, with examples, the similarities between the wine trade and the book trade. He also remarked that although he knew he should say he'd like to share the medal with his six great-grandchildren and the man who fixed his refrigerator, in fact he planned to take it home and use it to stroke his ego at regular intervals.

After he returned to Florida, he added a note to the folder of items he planned to discuss with me on my next visit: AMERICAN FREQ FLIER MILES TRANSFERABLE? He knew he'd never fly again and didn't want an unnecessary penny to be wasted.

Although his ambit was limited to Captiva, where he had no close friends, he was hardly a recluse. Using his Maxi-Aids phone, he called me several times a week. He called his brother Bill every Sunday. (A frequent topic of conversation was their brother Ed, who had died in a car accident twenty years earlier. My father still missed him.) And he spoke to Sam Aaron. When my father was eighty-

Me, my mother, my father (to whom she is a blur), and my husband, George Howe Colt, at the National Book Awards reception, 1993

six and Sam was seventy-eight, they had collaborated on a revised edition of *The Joys of Wine* in which my father declared himself still in love with wine, even if he was "now a Philemon rather than a Romeo." (Philemon and Baucis were a devoted old couple in Greek mythology who, when Zeus stopped by one evening, quenched his thirst with wine from a magical jug that was continually replenished. My father assumed everyone would know this.) Since then, Sam had developed glaucoma and become nearly as blind as my father. They commiserated on the phone, but mostly they talked about wine. Sam died of spinal cancer three years after my father lost his sight. I called with the news. My father wept, said goodbye, and called back twenty minutes later to dictate two hundred words he wished me to send to Sam's family. He said that Sam had taught him almost all he knew about wine, and that although most people keep their enthusiasm in a bank account, making withdrawals only when necessary, Sam "carried it with him and gave it away and yet the total sum was continually replenished."

When he was fifty-three, my father wrote:

> Our muscles give way at last to gravity's quiet, resistless pull; the best, the most joyful of our glands, in the end withers; the eye, the ear lose some of their fine quick power to seize upon the world; the limbs begin to ask What's the hurry? But I know men of eighty whose infirmities for a brief space of a bottle's emptying vanish as they sip their wine, their taste buds as lively as when they were one-and-twenty—nay, livelier.

Eighty sounded old to him then. When he was ninety, these words were even truer. He had had his share of losses: his brother, his best friend, his youth, his vigor, his influence, his sight. He had, in fact, lost everything, and more, that he had anticipated nearly four decades earlier when he turned the pages of his Cellar Book and thought about the two dark lines from *The Waste Land* that had puzzled me as a child:

> *London Bridge is falling down falling down falling*
> *   down . . .*
> *These fragments I have shored against my ruins . . .*

London Bridge *had* fallen down. But the fragments shored in his wine closet in Captiva (an even more modest depository than the one in Santa Barbara) were his purest source of pleasure, which was something he hadn't lost at all.

I once had a conversation over a good dinner with an elderly doctor who was writing a book on the factors that contribute to a satisfying old age. We agreed that the capacity for pleasure—especially the pleasure of taste—was high on the list. Gusto! Joie de vivre! The ability to eat, drink, and be merry, because tomorrow you really *are* going to die! Brillat-Savarin wrote that taste "invites us, by arousing our pleasure, to repair the constant losses which we suffer through our physical existence." He also wrote that it is "mathematically proven" that gourmands live longer. (He neglected to mention the mathematician.) My father had learned at VIP that the loss of one sense does not make the others more acute; he was annoyed by the popular assumption that every blind person has the nose of a bloodhound and the palate of an Escoffier. However, he *valued* his remaining senses more—sound and touch for utility, taste and smell for joy. Food was good. Wine was best: a miracle, because it was as good as it had ever been, which made it better. Anyone who wished to see wine truly being appreciated had only to watch my father oh-so-carefully convey a glass—a wavering blob of maroon or gold that got larger as it approached but never came into focus—to his nose, and then to his mouth.

I believe that the period between my father's first class at VIP and his final illness was in many ways one of the happiest of his life. This was in spite of his age; in spite of his losses; in spite of the moment every morning when he awoke from a dream in which he was invariably sighted, and then remembered he wasn't. It is said that old people can keep their minds agile by learning how to speak Italian or play the oboe. My father learned how to be blind. In the process, he may also have learned how to think of himself as a little less counterfeit, a little less like a seven-year-old who would never be as tall as his older brother. He had always worried that if he'd been the right age to serve in either world war, he would not have acquitted himself with honor. He had considered himself a coward. Now he knew he wasn't. *Mod sceal þe mare / þe ure mægen lytlað.*

And that's why I like to picture him sitting at his desk at ninety, without his glasses but with his blue checked shirt, his laugh wrinkles, his partially extant pompadour, and his beatific smile. He is probably wondering whether some of that good *pâté de campagne* is left for lunch, or whether the doorbell will be the FedEx man delivering a box of cassettes that might contain the next Great American Novel, or whether tonight, with the cheese tray, he and my mother—she'll have to uncork the bottle, but he's gotten used to that—should have the Simi Cabernet or break out the Chapelle-Chambertin. Hotsy totsy!

20

Impotence

Things don't always work out. Susannah Lescher, who relished the drop of Château d'Yquem that was placed on her tongue when she was six weeks old, is now a grown woman who realized long ago that she would never appreciate wine as much as her father did and now drinks only an occasional glass. Margaux Hemingway became an alcoholic, then a recovering alcoholic; three years before her suicide, she changed her name back to Margot. I was in my late forties when I finally admitted to myself that I would never love wine.

Improbable as it may seem, I didn't see it coming, but then I've never been good at noticing things right in front of me (keys, glasses, the black pants I am certain are not in the closet even though they must be in the closet). There was no single moment when I gave up for good; my hope just sort of faded away, like Gene Tunney's ectoplasmic wines or the fizz from a bottle of champagne with a crumbly cork.

I spent decades concealing the privileges of my childhood: the eight bathrooms, the varsity swimmer from UCLA who was hired to teach us the crawl, the servant-summoning bell above my mother's knee. I told people our family had lived in Westwood. It was really Bel Air. There. I've said it. I can never say Westwood again. I concealed my indifference to wine in similar fashion. As other women fake orgasms, I have faked hundreds of satisfied responses to hundreds of glasses of wine: not a difficult feat, since I could toss around the terms I learned as a child at the Fadiman dinner table (*pétillant*! phylloxera! Nebuchadnezzar!)—and then painstakingly direct the Bordeaux or Burgundy straight down the center of my tongue, a route that limited my palate's exposure to what it perceived as discomfiting intensity. But those days are over. Now that I have outed myself, I worry that no one will ever serve me wine again.

So I was happy to be invited not long ago to a mildly bibulous celebration at a friend's house in New Haven. Such formal occasions are rare. George and I left New York seventeen years ago, for more or less the same reasons my parents left California, and now live in rural western Massachusetts—not the swanky Berkshires but a farm town that produces apple cider, maple syrup, and parsnips. We have an old house and a couple of ramshackle barns with peeling paint. My anti-Arcadian father would have hated our place. But he would have loved that dinner: first-rate minds, first-rate food, enough WASPs to make him feel he'd crossed the river, enough Jews to make him feel he was not an outsider looking in.

The Far Niente Chardonnay '82 that accompanied the lobster ravioli was greeted with murmurs of quiet approbation. I found it . . . not unpleasant.

To accompany the glazed short ribs *sous vide*, my host brought out a Bordeaux. Before he removed the frail cork and decanted the wine, he showed me the bottle. It was an Haut-Brion '81.

An Haut-Brion?

We were about to drink one of the greatest wines in the world: one of the five *Premier Cru* Bordeaux, the only one made from grapes grown in the gravelly soil of Graves rather than in the nearby Médoc. I'd often noticed its label in one of the *Joys of Wine* gatefolds, embellished with an engraving of a château whose towers looked like witches' hats.

Haut-Brion is generally considered the first wine ever to receive a review—by the diarist Samuel Pepys, who visited London's Royall Oak Tavern on April 10, 1663 (one of at least six occasions that year on which he'd broken a wine-abstinence resolution), and, as he noted in his journal, "here drank a sort of French wine, called Ho Bryan, that hath a good and most particular taste that I never met with."

Haut-Brion appears in the wine cellar ledgers of King Charles II.

Haut-Brion was drunk by Dryden, Swift, Defoe, and Locke.

When Thomas Jefferson was the American minister to France, he bought six cases of Haut-Brion and sent them back to Monticello.

If ever a wine was a droplet of the river of human history, it was this one.

My host had bought the bottle twenty-five years earlier, at an end-of-term token price, from the Harvard Society of Fellows. The primary obligation of the junior fellows, of whom he was one, was to dine every Monday night with the senior fellows. The purpose of these weekly dinners was to bevel the young scholars' rough edges with conversation and buff them to a gloss with good wine. Wine as a civilizing agent: my father's credo.

My fellow guests took their first sips. Several broke out into a susurration of *mmmmm*s and *aaahhh*s and little grunts of pleasure.

I later looked up tasting notes for this Haut-Brion vintage—not a Great Year, but at the very least a good one, and in some estimations, very good or even magnificent. I read that other people had smelled coffee, cinnamon, nutmeg, tobacco, roses, violets, sour cherries, dried currants, star anise, white pepper, blue cheese, autumn leaves, saddle leather, iron filings, hot rocks in a cedar-paneled sauna, and earth. They had tasted pencil shavings, sandalwood, lavender, strawberries, plums, cassis, tea leaves, goat cheese, beef bouillon, green peppers, chocolate, vanilla, caramel, licorice, mint, peat, twigs, and toast.

I sniffed the wine. I couldn't smell any of those things, except earth.

I swallowed a drop.

It tasted—or so I imagined—like a muddy truffle that had been dug up moments earlier by a specially trained pig.

There are many things I don't want, but I don't want to want them. I wanted to want this. If I may transcend gender for a moment, there was only one word that came to mind: impotence. I felt the faintest stirrings of desire. I could tell I was in the presence of beauty—something complicated, intelligent, smoky, subterranean—but I could summon only the fragile ghost of a response.

When the next course came, half an inch of Haut-Brion was left in my glass.

If my father could read that sentence, he would weep.

21

Taste

In the months that followed the dinner in New Haven, I brooded about why I had left that half inch of Haut-Brion in the glass.

One day, during a phone conversation, a friend happened to mention that cilantro tastes different to different people. I looked it up and learned that cilantro-abomination is at least partly genetic. I happen to abominate cilantro. A surge of fellow feeling rose in me when I found a website called IHateCilantro.com, on which one of my gustatory brethren had posted the following admirable haiku:

> *Hated, vile, foul herb*
> *One mere leaf destroys the meal.*
> *Oh, to be tongueless!*

Others described the object of our mutual disaffection as tasting like old soap, moldy carpet, dirty laundry, toilet cleaner, dish detergent, paint thinner, furniture polish, Scotch tape, burnt rubber, wet dog, cat piss, skunk spray, ear wax, doll hair, baby wipes, damp socks, moldy shoes, old coins, stink bugs, feet wrapped in bacon, and "a cigarette if you ate it."

I had never eaten a cigarette, but I felt sure that if I had, I would have recognized the incontestable rightness of the comparison, as I did the others. The sandalwood and lavender lurking in a glass of Haut-Brion may have eluded me, but when it came to cilantro, I was on firm ground. Old soap—yes! Moldy shoes—totally! Feet wrapped in bacon—amen! These were tasting notes I could get behind.

The seed of a radical new thought had been planted. What if wine was sort of like cilantro? Though I didn't abominate wine, I certainly didn't appreciate it. What if the sense that had given my father more pleasure than any other was wired differently in his daughter, in which case there was no way she could like exactly what he liked? Maybe wine was a blind spot not because I was morally, emotionally, intellectually, or aesthetically deficient but because I was *biologically* deficient. That would get me off the hook, wouldn't it? I'd be like someone who doesn't enjoy reading not because she's uncultivated but because she's dyslexic.

I started thinking about other foods I didn't like. Capers. Kimchi. Cloves. Pepper. Kale. Coffee was drinkable—in fact, positively delicious—only with milk and sugar. Seltzer required enough discreet mouth-sloshing to subdue the effervescence. And I couldn't imagine why anyone would eat a radish unless paid. It was more like a bee-sting than a vegetable.

What did these foods have in common with the way wine tasted to me (which was to say sort of sour, sort of bitter, pucker-inducing, not just a taste but a sensation)? They were all too strong. And to whom did foods taste too strong? Supertasters.

I had come across the word when I looked up cilantro. You couldn't read an article on taste without bumping into it. There was even an indie rock song called "John Lee Supertaster," which contained the memorable lines "When he tastes a pear / It's like a hundred pears." (The backup singers croon in response, "It's like a *million* pears.") According to Linda Bartoshuk, the taste scientist who coined the term in 1991, supertasters were people for whom salt tasted saltier, sugar tasted sweeter, pickles tasted more sour, chard tasted more bitter, and Worcestershire sauce tasted umami-er. (Umami, the so-called fifth taste, is the meaty or savory flavor imparted by glutamate.) Their tongues had more—lots more—fungiform papillae, the little mushroom-shaped bumps that house the taste buds. As King Arthur was identified by pulling a sword from a stone and witches were identified by being bound and dunked, supertasters could be identified by either counting their papillae or placing on their tongues a filter-paper disk soaked in 6-*n*-propylthiouracil, a chemical used to treat hyperthyroidism, otherwise known as PROP. To 25 percent of the population, the non-tasters, the disk tastes like nothing. ("Non-taster" is a misnomer. Everyone can taste PROP, but not everyone can taste it at very low concentrations.) To 50 percent, the medium tasters, it tastes bitter. To the remaining 25 percent, the supertasters, it tastes so terrible that one unfortunate consumer said his tongue thrashed around his mouth like a hooked fish convulsing on the deck of a boat.

One might expect that wine connoisseurs—those people who confidently call a Syrah "peppery" or a Pinot Noir–based champagne "biscuity"—would possess the papillae to which a pear tastes like a million pears. That isn't necessarily the case. Supertasting may be a liability. If you experience bitterness, astringency, acidity, and alcohol (which is sensed as heat) far more intensely than an ordinary mortal, you may find it hard to enjoy wines that are tannic or tart or have a high alcohol content. You want less. If you're a non-taster, on the other hand, you want more. You have to clobber your palate in order to feel you're tasting much of anything and are at greater risk of becoming an alcoholic because you don't dislike the taste of alcohol. The Goldilocks *via media* is happily occupied by the medium tasters. I couldn't resurrect my father in order to ply him with PROP-impregnated paper and see if his tongue thrashed, but I'd have bet my unabridged *OED* that he was a medium taster and I was a supertaster.

Supertaster: Now there was an identity I could get used to. I was a delicate flower whose hyper-refined sensibilities were assailed by the crude world! I was off the hook, but not because I was dyslexic; my problem was that I read too well! I liked wine less than my father did because my palate was *superior*! I resolved to confirm my rarefied status without delay.

I didn't yet know that not all taste scientists view PROP as the alpha and omega of gustatory assessment. Although Linda Bartoshuk found that responses to PROP correlated strongly with papilla density, as well as with many other aspects of taste perception, some of her critics have pointed out that it is possible to be insensitive to PROP but have receptors that can taste many other bitter compounds; that taste sensitivity depends on the response to a variety of stimuli; and that PROP testing ignores the role of smell in taste perception. In any case, I couldn't find PROP online, so I sent away for a strip flavored with phenylthiocarbamide, PROP's chemical cousin. After it arrived, I read that PTC is poisonous (one website reported that, pound for pound, it was "safer than a poison dart frog, but deadlier than strychnine"). Although .005 milligrams would probably not have done me in, I retreated to Plan B: counting my fungiform papillae.

The word "fungiform" was new to me. So were "foliate" and "circumvallate," two kinds of papillae located elsewhere on the tongue and in the mouth and throat, both crucial to taste though less easy to see and thus not employed in supertaster testing. But "papillae" was an old friend. When Kim and I were in middle school, we had entered a jingle contest sponsored by Dr Pepper. Our collaborative offering:

Dr Pepper has a zest
Which makes it far the tastiest.
So buy a bottle, make the test!
Your papillae will do the rest.

Kim, who had a larger vocabulary than I did, was responsible for "papillae." We were astonished and out-
raged when we didn't win.

Following online instructions, I used a Q-tip to stain
my tongue blue with food coloring. Its spongy surface
would allegedly absorb the dye while the fungiform papillae remained pink and prominent. I placed a gummed
reinforcement on the middle of my tongue. My mission
was to count the rosy bumps that lay within the reinforcement's six-millimeter circle: non-tasters had fewer
than fifteen, medium tasters fifteen to thirty-five, and
supertasters more than thirty-five. Unfortunately, the
mirror fogged up every time I leaned in close, and even
when I wiped a patch clear for a few seconds, my middle-
aged eyes could no more distinguish an individual papilla than they could a neutrino. I tried reading glasses, a
magnifying glass, and a flashlight. No dice. I tried my
husband. He couldn't see anything either. Finally, I con-
scripted my college-age daughter and stuck out my bright
blue tongue.

She counted five papillae.

Five! Oh my God. Could I be—I could hardly say it to
myself—a *non-taster*? It wasn't possible. I always did well
on tests. Perhaps I had placed the reinforcement in a less
than optimal spot on my tongue, a sort of papillary Sahara.

I moved it toward the front. Susannah counted eighteen.

I moved it to the very center of the tip. Twenty-five.

Better. Still, not what I'd had in mind. Instead of being incomparably sensitive, was my palate smack in the middle of medium?

Smarting from my demotion, I decided to pay a visit to Virginia Utermohlen, the former director of the Cornell Taste Science Laboratory and an authority on individual differences in taste sensitivity. I was interested in her claim that she has saved marriages by proving that spouses with divergent food preferences are not being fussy or stubborn; they simply live in different perceptual universes. I'd also enjoyed a paper in which she persuasively argued that Marcel Proust could probably taste 6-n-propylthiouracil.

When I arrived in Ithaca, I wasn't sure why she had reserved a table at a wine and tapas bar. I wanted to talk about wine, not drink it. However, I was delighted by Dr. Utermohlen, who looked exactly the way a taste scientist should: pink-cheeked and round, as if she'd spent her life eating delicious foods, which indeed turned out to be the case. She immediately affixed her white cloth napkin to a necklace equipped with two alligator clips, a gift from a relative who had noticed that she ate with such enthusiasm that she often spilled her soup. She then ordered us each a flight of five local wines from the Finger Lakes region: a Hermann J. Wiemer Cuvée Brut, a Treleaven Chardonnay, a Charles Fournier Gold Seal Vineyards Riesling, a Hazlitt 1852 Vineyards Sauvignon

Blanc, and a Bellwether Sawmill Creek Vineyard Pinot Noir. I had told her beforehand that wine tasted overly strong to me, and she had told me that it did to her, too. In order to reduce its intensity, she swallowed wine down the center of her tongue, *just like me.*

Soon, along with several plates of tapas, our table was occupied by a brigade of tiny glasses. I cautiously sipped from each of them.

With the exception of the Sauvignon Blanc, they were—well, much better than I expected.

Dr. Utermohlen said, "Of course they are." She explained that at this northern latitude the growing season was shorter, the grapes developed less sugar to ferment, and the lower sugar levels meant less alcohol. The alcohol content of these wines was between 11 and 12.5 percent, well below the 14 or 15 percent that is now common in California. "You don't like alcohol," she said. "This is your wine country."

The Sauvignon Blanc tasted bitter. "Methoxypyrazine," she said. "That's the Cabernet signature. How do you feel about green peppers?" I told her I preferred red and yellow ones. "Of course you do," she said. "The green ones have methoxypyrazine, just like this wine."

The Pinot Noir was my favorite. "Of course it is," she said. She explained that, compared with the Cabernet, it was lighter in every way: body, flavor, tannin, color. Pinot Noirs tend to be low in pigment because they are made from thin-skinned grapes, but the cool climate and long winters of the Finger Lakes give the grape skins an especially brief opportunity to develop color, and the resulting wines are pale and delicate. Was it possible that I preferred this anemic-looking red—perilously close to a rosé, my father's *bête noire*—to the Haut-Brion I had tasted in New Haven? Thomas Jefferson would never have bought six cases. But I had to admit that it was sort of pleasant.

For a moment, a flicker of hope stirred within my fungiform papillae. Might these unintimidating wines serve as training wheels? Could I eventually graduate to Haut-Brion?

The flicker didn't last long. "Sort of pleasant" was unbridgeably distant from "bottled poetry" (Robert Louis Stevenson), "constant proof that God loves us" (Benjamin Franklin), and "one of the indices of civilization" (Clifton Fadiman, who makes at least one appearance in every list of wine quotations).

After dinner, Dr. Utermohlen—who had grown even pinker because, as she explained, she has an acetaldehyde dehydrogenase deficiency that causes her to flush when she drinks alcohol—drove me to an ice cream parlor where she was obviously well known. I had a large dish of Mint Chocolate Chip and Chocolate Bittersweet. She had a kiddie-sized scoop of Pumpkin in a sugar cone. We agreed that the wines had been pretty good but the ice cream was better. Had my father been present at Purity Ice Cream that evening, he would not have been pleased. He once wrote that watching adults drink ice cream sodas gave him "the same queasy feeling one gets from watching an adult playing with a rattle in a lunatic asylum." Dr. Utermohlen would have had an excellent rejoinder. She'd told me at dinner that children avoid bitter and sour flavors because they have far more sensitive palates than adults. Their tastes change not because their palates improve but because they deteriorate.

The next day, Dr. Utermohlen photographed my tongue with her iPhone. She wasn't interested in a six-millimeter circle; she wanted the big picture. "It's a beautiful tongue," she said. "It's exquisite." She zoomed in on the image and showed me a forest of fungiform papillae, including many, tucked into an inch-long fissure, that might not have been visible at home because, as she explained, fissures have a high concentration of papillae but tend to absorb food coloring. "You've got a ton of papillae—a ton, a ton, a ton. And look at how many you have on the side! An insane quantity. That's why you swallow wine down the center. You are highly sensitive."

My first realization was that I'd been mispronouncing "papillae" for nearly half a century. I'd never heard anyone say it until that moment and had always thought the accent was on the first syllable, not the second. No wonder Kim and I had lost the Dr Pepper jingle contest! My second realization was that Dr. Utermohlen had just snatched my tongue from the jaws of mediocrity.

However, she had called me merely "highly sensitive"; she had not used the word "supertaster." I had an inkling why after I asked if I could see *her* tongue. Out it came, a very pink, very clean tongue, so extravagantly fissured that it deserved its own topographic map. It was the tongue of an imperial supertaster. My tongue was not in the same league. (She later confided that she could detect

PROP at a concentration of one part per billion, though she belongs to the camp of taste scientists who believe that its importance has been exaggerated. She actually *prefers* the term "highly sensitive taster," which encompasses the tasting cosmos beyond PROP.)

Dr. Utermohlen confirmed her assessment by instructing me to think about a favorite meal in order to stimulate salivation (spinach ravioli), place a peppermint Life Saver in my mouth, wait till it softened, crunch it, and rate the intensity of the taste and the rush of coolness. They were both strong. She explained that the rush, which not everyone feels, came from the activation of the trigeminal nerve endings in my mouth and nose. Taste is transmitted not only by the papillae but by the trigeminal nerve, which carries sensations of heat, cold, astringency, pungency, pain, and prickle. Menthol activates the same taste receptors that sense cold temperatures, so we perceive it as cold; the same is true for capsaicin (the active component in chili peppers) and heat. Carbonated beverages activate prickle receptors: a matter of mouthfeel, which combines with taste and aroma to form the complete profile of a food's flavor.

She then brought me a cup of strong green tea. Bitter! And unpleasantly astringent, even several seconds later. Before the next sip, I swallowed a teaspoon of sugar, and before the third sip, a pinch of salt. In each case the tea tasted milder, even though the sugar and salt were no longer in my mouth when I drank it. Dr. Utermohlen told me that both sugar and salt prevent bitter and astringent compounds from binding to taste receptors, and that their effects linger after they are swallowed. Salt is especially effective, which explained why, like most highly sensitive tasters (the term was starting to grow on me), I often wanted more of it even though I wanted less of almost everything else.

After asking a battery of questions about my flavor preferences (Do you like your chili hot? How are you with Listerine?) as well as my father's (Did he like parmesan? Did he drink his coffee black?), Dr. Utermohlen drew a chart of the spectrum of some major oral receptors, protein molecules that unlock specific ion channels in nerve cells and allow particular tastes and sensations to be perceived. On the left were the "cold" receptors, TRPA1 (transient receptor potential, subfamily A, member 1) and TRPM8. On the right was the "hot" receptor, TRPV1. Both extremes caused pain. Capsaicin and alcohol, sensed by TRPV1, could burn; so could wasabi, which, to my surprise, was sensed by TRPA1, a receptor that responds both to unpleasantly cold temperatures and to pungent compounds in the mustard family. (I dislike hot chili but like wasabi.) In between lay TRPM5 and TRPV3. All the foods I enjoyed were sensed by the three receptors on the left: the cool side. All the ones I didn't were on the right: the hot side. My father's favorite foods were concentrated in the center and near right. Dr. Utermohlen said that he was probably highly sensitive at the level of the taste buds but less sensitive at the level of the trigeminal nerve. I was highly sensitive at both. I would prefer low-tannin, low-oak wines on the cooler side of the spectrum, like last night's Pinot Noir, though even they might seem too sour or too bitter. "Your father had the perfect palate for wine," she said. "The way wine was then. Lower alcohol content, higher residual sugar. The classic Bordeaux. He wouldn't have liked today's big reds, over on the right: too much alcohol burn."

Before I left, Dr. Utermohlen told me that the tongue inspection, the Life Saver test, and the taste questions had not been strictly necessary. She'd known the previous night what kind of taster I was because I had been interested in only a few things on the tapas menu (I'd shuddered at the thought of the Warm Baby Kale with Goat Cheese Vinaigrette, Beets, Walnuts, Pickled Onion, and Radish), but the ones I'd wanted (particularly the Saffron Risotto Cake Stuffed with Fontina Cheese, with Grilled Ramps and Sliced Tomato) I'd *really* wanted. "That's what we've found with the highly sensitive tasters," she said. "They have loves and hates." She explained that the beloved foods inspire such rapture that first bites are remembered decades later; the hated foods are viewed as invaders that must be vigilantly barred from entering the body, even in minute quantities. That's exactly how I feel. Dr. Utermohlen's own loves include empanadas ("but not with peas"), artichokes ("but not the hearts"), spinach ("Oh my God"), coffee mousse ("straight from heaven"), and cinnamon ("I like a little TRPV1"). Her hates— "Holy mackerel! Hate, hate, hate!"—include hazelnuts, goat cheese, Brussels sprouts, peaches, and rice pudding. She dislikes going to other people's houses for dinner because she's afraid of encountering one of her hates, about which the host or hostess will invariably say, "The way I cook it, you'll love it." That, of course, is invariably untrue. Dr. Utermohlen left me with the impression that the term "picky eater" was invented by people with fewer papillae in order to diss people with more papillae.

A few weeks later I spent an afternoon with Larry Marks, a scientist who studies sensory perception at the John B. Pierce Laboratory at Yale. Dr. Marks was a distinguished gray-haired man who looked far too thin to be a taste researcher (and indeed had also published work on synesthesia and ventriloquism). He told me his three basic food groups were black coffee, dark chocolate, and red wine, starting with Thunderbird at seventeen and working his way up to Côtes du Rhône.

Dr. Marks led me to a table on which sixty tiny plastic cups, each containing 5 cc of clear liquid, had been arrayed in precise rows, as if for an unusually well-organized game of beer pong. First came the "gustation test." The thirty cups on the left contained either plain water or water with very low concentrations—undetectable by some people, unidentifiable by many—of salt, sucrose, citric acid, quinine, or MSG. Following Dr. Marks's instructions, I swirled the contents of each cup in my mouth, spat into a dedicated sink that had received the expectorate of countless tasters before me, rinsed with water, and moved on to the next cup: more or less like a wine tasting, but without the wine. I wrote down whether each sample tasted salty, sweet, sour, bitter, umami, or flavorless.

The thirty cups on the right contained either water or a very weak solution of blueberry, strawberry, peach, banana, or vanilla flavoring. They constituted an "olfaction test," a term that led me to assume, incorrectly, that I'd be sniffing them. Instead, I was instructed to hold my breath, place each liquid in my mouth for a few seconds, and then spit it out. I couldn't taste a thing until I exhaled, at which point I apparently experienced each flavor as its vapors wafted up my pharynx and into my nose. I dislike—in some cases, like Dr. Utermohlen, hate, hate, hate!—many fruits, and had not eaten a peach or a banana since I was a child, though I had smelled them, with displeasure, when others had eaten them in my presence. I did not expect to recognize these flavors, and when I did I wished I hadn't, even though they were the faintest of zephyrs.

After I'd completed both tests, Dr. Marks extended his hand, as if proffering an after-dinner mint. He was holding an envelope that contained several small white disks. PROP! I'd finally found it. Even though I knew that the trials I'd just undergone might be a more complete predictor of taste sensitivity, it still vibrated with talismanic power.

I placed a disk on my tongue.

Ewwwwwwwwww.

It was the bitterest substance I had tasted in my entire life. And the bitterness lingered, even after I had plucked the offending scrap of filter paper from my mouth.

Dr. Marks handed me a piece of paper with a graduated line on which seven levels of sensory intensity were marked and labeled. The instructions, though only one sentence long, were epic in scope: "Please rate in the context of the full range of sensations that you have experienced in your life."

All sensations? Well, childbirth was worse. Also, to be fair, my tongue had not thrashed like a hooked fish. I drew a mark partway between the top two levels, "Very Strong" and "Strongest Imaginable."

A lab assistant brought in the score sheets from the earlier tests, and Dr. Marks summarized my results. In the gustation test, I had been unable to distinguish between the salty and the umami samples, but I had correctly identified four of the five water samples, four of the five sour samples, and all five bitter samples. In other words, I was sensitive to sourness and very sensitive to bitterness. In the olfaction test, I had correctly identified twenty-eight of thirty samples, including all ten samples of the flavors I hadn't tasted in decades. I was exceptionally sensitive. In the PROP test, I was exactly on the border between medium taster and supertaster. *So close and yet so far!* (Dr. Marks told me he was on the border between non-taster and medium taster himself: he could tell that PROP was bitter, but just barely. No wonder he liked black coffee.)

Dr. Marks had been trained as a cognitive psychologist, and he cautioned me to remember that biology is not the sole determinant of taste preferences. Experience matters too. For instance, he noted that if a child grows up in Mexico and starts eating chili peppers as a toddler, she'll get used to them, and probably even learn to enjoy them, whether or not she was initially sensitive to capsaicin. However, he had no doubt that my sensitivity to bitterness was responsible for my dislike of wines with high tannin levels—the more tannins, the more I'd balk. I asked him why, if I was so good at distinguishing flavors, I wasn't better at telling wines apart. He explained that it was partly a matter of practice—I just hadn't drunk enough—and partly because my general sensitivity overwhelmed my capacity to discriminate.

My sensitivity to bitterness was later reconfirmed after I ordered a kit from 23andMe, a genetic testing company, and spat into a little plastic tube. I was duly informed that I had several variants—none of them particularly rare—in TAS2R38 and TAS2R13, two of the genes that encode for the taste receptors that perceive bitterness. One set of variants intensifies the perception of bitter flavors in general, including PROP; the other specifically intensifies the perception of bitterness in alcohol. All the variants were heterozygous, which meant I had inherited them from only one parent (I feel pretty sure it was the milk-shake lover) and not from the other (the wine lover).

So there it was. I didn't taste what my father tasted.

This knowledge made me both happy and sad. It was a relief to know that I might not be such an anhedonic stick-in-the-mud after all. I wished I'd met Dr. Utermohlen and Dr. Marks years ago. I would have felt, if not completely exonerated, at least less convinced that my inability to appreciate wine was a character flaw.

But it wasn't exactly *good* news. It made me feel like a child with a palate so finicky that she is doomed to eat only Nilla Wafers. Forever.

Or a woman who is doomed to drink Pinot Grigio, the perennial darling of ladies' luncheons, and Merlot, or, as the wine snob in *Sideways* called it, "fucking Merlot." That's the advice I was given by myVinotype, an online quiz created by one of Dr. Utermohlen's colleagues, a taste researcher named Tim Hanni. After answering a brief series of questions about my food preferences (one of which was whether I hated cilantro), I was informed that my "Vinotype Persona" was Hypersensitive, which seemed to be code for "has pathetic taste in wines." Hanni believes that wine stores should organize their bottles not by origin and varietal but by alcohol content and intensity of flavor, and that every sommelier should learn to assess a diner's taste sensitivity and recommend wines accordingly. He may be right. But I'm stuck. The only wines I might want to drink are the ones I would never want to drink.

Not long after my taste tests, I had dinner with two writers. One of them, a wine critic, brought a Beaune Les Avaux 2001, a *Premier Cru* Burgundy; the other, a poet, brought a Montepulciano d'Abruzzo, a rustic red from central Italy that looked nearly opaque. I tried the Beaune. The usual. Too strong. The wine critic was disappointed; he had thought, as everyone always does, that even if I didn't like wine, I'd like *this* wine. I didn't dare even try the Montepulciano. I knew it would knock me to the floor. After hearing about my exquisite papillae and my off-the-charts olfaction score, the poet said, "You're like an Empath!" Empaths are inordinately sensitive humanoids or human-humanoid hybrids on *Star Trek*, one of whom suffers horribly when she absorbs the pain of

Captain Kirk and Dr. McCoy on a mission in the Minarian star system. The poet wasn't giving me a compliment; she was expressing sympathy.

One night, as I was looking at a diagram of a tongue on my laptop screen, I thought to myself, *My father would have hated all this.* Not because he disliked science; he had enjoyed reading biographies of scientists and edited two anthologies of stories and poems about mathematics. But he would have thought that "fungiform" and "circumvallate" were ugly words—words that Wally the Wordworm would never have wanted to eat. He would have felt that reducing wine to a series of tests and charts and genetic acronyms would be like feeding a Keats sonnet into a computer and spitting out an analysis of metrics and phonemes, or grinding up Chartres Cathedral in order to weigh the stone and the glass.

My father wrote that wine contains "an inexplicable *élan vital*." Inexplicable. It not only couldn't be explained, it shouldn't be. He would not have wanted to know which trigeminal receptors he had used to taste the Château Lafite Rothschild 1904 at his eightieth-birthday lunch, just as he would not have wanted to read a chemist's account of how it had been produced. He liked to think of wine as made partly by human beings but mostly by the glorious lottery of soil and slope and sun and rainfall, no two vineyards alike, no two years alike, no two bottles alike, the whole enterprise risky, suspenseful, and at least partly accidental.

"Accidental" is another word for "miraculous." If the

opposite of science is religion, then my father's feelings about wine were as religious as he ever got. He wrote that "wine drinking is like music or mysticism. All three are in the end inexpressible by words." (His own wine essays, including the one that contained that phrase, proved him wrong.) He compared the impossibility of writing about wine to the impossibility of writing about "the sensation of union with the Divine." Although he thought Catholicism was foolish, he was moved by the Eucharist: to call wine the blood of Christ was to acknowledge its inestimable value.

My researches made me feel different from my father not only in matters of gustation and olfaction but also in character. He liked to leave some things a mystery. I'd rather find everything out.

In matters of wine non-appreciation, I have discovered I am far from alone. Everywhere I go these days I seem to run into people who belong to the club. Its members include two former students of mine, one who says that half a glass leaves her zonked and red-faced (I suspect an acetaldehyde dehydrogenase deficiency) and another who invests in wine futures—specifically, 2003 Château Pontet-Canet—but has never sampled his stock because he says wine makes his mouth hurt (trigeminal sensitivity). And my old Sedgwick boyfriend recently told me that his late father, who could easily have afforded Château Pontet-Canet, opted for half-gallon bottles of S. S. Pierce Sauternes, into which he stirred half a cup of sugar (genetic variant for sweet preference).

And, of course, there's my brother Kim. After I received the results of my 23andMe test, I called to tell him about TAS2R38 and TAS2R13. I thought he might want to send off a saliva sample himself, but he didn't. Like our father, he finds data reductive. Also, he'd already told me why he thought neither of us liked wine. I asked him years ago. He said, "Because we didn't need to escape our origins."

22

Memorabilia

My father didn't leave much behind. A favorite family story involved Kim, at age two, watching him sit down at the breakfast table in a foul humor, and relieving the tension by shouting, from his high chair, "Throw everything out, Daddy!" The only material possession my father treasured was the giant copper wastebasket under his desk. To lighten his load when he traveled, he dismembered paperback books and discarded the pages he'd already read. Once, in an insomniac funk, he wrote, "It is selfish and I have been taught not to do it, but what paradise to die in possession of nothing but your own death-sweat." He just about managed it.

He had once wanted to leave us only books and wine, which he considered not objects but experiences. More than a thousand of his books are now on my shelves, including twenty or so *about* wine. I consulted them when I wrote these pages. His wine was gone before he was. He had never expected to live long enough to drink it all, or to have children who wouldn't have wanted it even if there had been any left to inherit. My wine cellar consists of the two empty bottles in my study—the 1835 Madeira once owned by Elbridge T. Gerry, Jr., and the 1904 Château Lafite Rothschild we drank at the Book-of-the-Month Club on his eightieth birthday—and one full bottle, a 1981 Boyer Brut Blanc de Blancs, Cuvée Fadiman, from the Four Seasons dinner, with the photograph of my father on the label. I've been waiting for the right moment to open it. I'd use my father's butterfly corkscrew, now mine, the one I saw him plunge and twirl and twist nearly every night of my childhood, though the auger is now rusty and the brass levers are stippled with verdigris. Drinking the Cuvée Fadiman might feel a trifle cannibalistic, like a Papua New Guinea tribesman incorporating the essence of his late father by eating him, but perhaps I would incorporate some of my father's finer qualities, such as neatness and a constitutional inability to misuse a preposition. Unfortunately, the bottle is now thirty-three years old, a geriatric age for a white. Not enough tannins. And of course there's that other problem: I probably wouldn't like it anyway.

In his last years, with the help of his secretary's eyes, my father gradually thinned his files until only what he considered essential—mostly medical, legal, and financial documents—remained. Everything else was dispatched to the copper wastebasket, which now sits under my own desk. The folders that survived the cull used to fit into a single lateral drawer in his Captiva study and now occupy a single lateral drawer in my study in Massachusetts. You might think that I would have read every page as soon as the boxes were delivered, hungrily sniffing out every last vestige of him, but I didn't. Going through a dead parent's memorabilia is a hazardous undertaking; there is a fine line between pleasure and pain. I enjoyed the CORRESPONDENCE folders (letters from eighty-seven famous or once-famous people, mostly writers, including W. H. Auden, Pearl S. Buck, Edna Ferber, M.F.K. Fisher, Ralph Ellison, Aldous Huxley, Alfred Kazin, Arthur Koestler, Walker Percy, Mary Renault, William Saroyan, Stephen Spender, James Thurber, Robert Penn Warren, E. B. White, and Thornton Wilder—an entire literary generation—that had been spared the copper wastebasket only because it dawned on my father around 1960 that they might be worth something). But I ran aground on FADIMAN, ANNE. Although he never kept copies of his own letters and had thrown out all the drafts of his own writing, he had kept twelve alphabetized folders containing my essays and articles, my report cards back to the sixth grade, all my letters (including the ones I sent from France when I was fifteen), and POST-TONSILLECTOMY WRITINGS (the notes I had passed him, unable to speak, while he read me *War and Peace*).

It was a long time before I felt able to press on through FIDELITY BROKERAGE SERVICES, MEDICAL PLAN INFO, and STATE FARM AUTO INSURANCE, all the way to the end of the alphabet. I'd started working on this book and knew I had to look at everything. Near the end of the drawer, squeezed between WILLS, INCL. CODI-CILS and WORLD POETRY, there was a folder I had never noticed, because it was bulgier than its neighbors and had sunk half an inch below them, concealing its tab. The tab said WINE MEMORABILIA.

I remember exactly where I was standing when I opened the folder. I placed it on top of the low bookcase that held the *Encyclopædia Britannica* my father had given me long before the Internet existed. (As a member of its Board of Editors, he got an employee discount.) I was surrounded by the books and papers I used in my job teaching in an Ivy League English department: the very thing he had most wanted to do himself. It was after dinner on a warm summer night. I was facing west.

The folder contained a wine list, a menu, a magazine article, and his Cellar Book.

His Cellar Book.

I could practically recite the sentence in "Brief History of a Love Affair," which I had reread countless times, that followed his description of his "happy marriage" with wine: "The record of our union is contained in my Cellar Book, the earliest entry being that of October 17, 1935, at which time I seem to have laid down a dozen Morey, Clos des Lambrays '29 at a price ($28) that today induces wistful dreams. 'Quite beautiful' is the notation under 'Remarks.'"

This was it. The record of their union. It was like finding a sheaf of old love letters.

My father's Cellar Book was not exactly a book; it was a mismatched collection of documents with overlapping and missing dates. There were loose pages of various shapes and sizes, the paper foxed and some of the margins Scotch-taped, with entries from 1935 to 1950. The first six of those pages had been torn from the back of a wine book to which they served as a kind of appendix. (I later discovered that it was none other than Schoonmaker and Marvel's *Complete Wine Book*, which my father had published at Simon & Schuster the previous year. True to form, he'd jettisoned the rest of the book.) There was also a 3¾-by-5-inch "Wine Account"— maroon leather covers, blue marbled endpapers, gilt-edged pages—with entries from 1948 to 1950. In his familiar handwriting, my father had recorded in these miscellaneous logs each wine he bought, along with the vintage, the number of bottles, the date, the storage location, and sometimes a tasting note. The loose pages made little protesting sounds as I pried apart the Scotch tape, which was glossy—it predated Magic Tape by decades— and yellowed to near-opacity. The leather Wine Account, which had caused the WINE MEMORABILIA folder to bulge in the middle and sink below the other files in the drawer, smelled ancient and fragile, as if I'd opened a fine Bordeaux so old its cork might crumble.

I knew what the first entry was going to be: Morey, Clos des Lambrays '29. There it was. Twelve bottles, $28. But I was surprised to see that the date on the first line wasn't 10/17/35; it was 12/17/35. Five December entries were followed by a long series of October entries. It took me a few minutes to understand that my father had begun his Cellar Book near the end of the year but

Class of Wine and Growth	Year	Name of Shipper	Quantity Purchased	Date Purchased
*Morey, Clos des Lambrays	'29		12	12/17/35
*Chat. Pichon-Longueville	'29		6	"
*Charmes-Chambertin	29		6	"
Clos-Vougeot	21		1	12/26/35
Chat Pavie	29		1	"
Monthelie	'29		1	10/18/35
Charmes-Chambertin	'29		1	"
Volnay Clos des Framiet	'29		1	"
Morey, Clos des Lambrays	'29		1	"
Chablis, Valmur	'28		1	"
Pouilly, Tête de Cavée	'28		1	"
Corton, Clos du Roi	'28		1/2	"
Tritten heimer Neuberg	'33		1/2	"
Piesporter Gold-Tropfel	'29		1	"

Name of Dealer	Price Paid	Remarks	Date
B & S	28 —		
"	11 —		
"	12.50		
		From Parker Morell — UWO the finest description I ever tasted	
"	" BH		
	sold to Bill		
"	18 —	Passable	
"	25 —	good	
"	27 —	Beautiful, perfectly balanced will improve	
"	28 —	Quite beautiful	
"	22.50	Refreshing & insistently genuine — worth buying	
"	20. —	Almost as good as above; and very similar	
"	29 —	Excellent (good to stock)	
"	17.50		
"	26. —	too young	

The opening pages of the Cellar Book, 1935

had recorded his earlier purchases as well. He'd made a minor mistake in "Brief History of a Love Affair": he'd actually started collecting wine not on October 17 but on October 18, 1935, when his acquisitions had also included a case of Clos des Lambrays (its quantity recorded not as "12" bottles but as "1" case)—one that had indeed been "Quite beautiful." Or, rather, "Quite Beautiful." When he made the notation, he'd been so excited he'd capitalized the *B*.

Looking at the real thing was different from reading about it. My father's essay had removed all the complications, and also much of the flavor.

As I leafed through the pages, I recognized all the great names from my childhood, some of them in the company of Great Years. There were the *Premier Cru* Bordeaux. Château Margaux '29 (first laid down 10/18/35, one case, $25). Château Latour, '28 (first laid down 12/23/36, a gift). Château Haut-Brion '26 (first laid down 10/1/37, one bottle, $1.95). Château Lafite Rothschild '28 (first laid down 4/7/37, one bottle, $1.75); my father noted that it had "turned" and was replaced ten days later with a second, more satisfactory bottle. Château Mouton Rothschild '28 (first laid down 3/10/36, two bottles, $2.35 each). There were several of the *Grand Cru* Burgundies I'd learned to recognize by the time I was in the sixth grade. Chambertin '29 (first laid down 10/1/37, one bottle, $1.65). Montrachet '29 (first laid down 10/1/37, six bottles, $1.65 each). Grands Échézeaux '33 (first laid down 10/1/41, one case, $35.40). There was Château d'Yquem '25 (first laid down 4/18/36, a gift). Holy Moses, there was Château Branaire-Ducru, the so-obscure-it-should-have-been-impossible-to-guess claret from the Roald Dahl story about the wagered daughter! This one was a '29 (first laid down 10/18/35, one case, $17.50).

The proper nouns induced a sensation somewhere between shivering and crying. I could remember only one other time I'd felt like that. Two decades earlier, I had written a profile of a Nebraska monk. I had asked what the monastic tradition offered him to compensate for giving up the company of women. He answered by reciting, without further explanation, the names of the fabled medieval abbeys: Tintern. Cîteaux. Wearmouth-Jarrow. Lindisfarne. Fountains. Rievaulx.

Great names.

Lindisfarne and Grands Échézeaux conjured worlds that were old and noble and beautiful. I might not wish to *participate*—chant matins at 4:00 a.m., swallow the Burgundy—but the words made me want to fall to my knees.

My father did not comment on every wine in his Cellar Book. The most famous bottles were often recorded without annotation, as if assessments would profane them, though he did remark that a Clos de Vougeot '21—from the vineyard that Napoleon's soldiers were commanded to salute as they marched past—was "one of the finest Burgundies I have ever tasted." When he made a note, it was brief and confident. "Gorgeous." "Insipid." "Passable." "Superb!" "Bigness, no greatness; but very satisfactory." "Lovely; ready now." "Still hard; wait." "Great breeding + suavity; might be still better in five years." "Sound, good nose, but a little thin." "Young, green, mediocre."

"Trifle faded." "Too quininy." "Touch of acid; '26's not keeping." "Pleasant little affair." "Swell."

There may have been some blank spaces under "Remarks," but never under "Price Paid." My father and money: always a tight couple. The Cellar Book, which was laid out in double-page spreads with vertical columns, looked a lot like the spreadsheets on which he kept track of his stocks. I could tell how much pleasure he had taken in filling in the prices. Every dollar sign said *I can afford this. I know about this. I am going to enjoy this.* It was like a bank book. These wines were his life's savings.

On the first day of his new life as a wine collector, he bought *nine hundred and eight bottles*. He spent well over a thousand dollars, the equivalent of more than fifteen thousand dollars today. That was a wild spree— undoubtedly one of the largest expenditures he'd ever made—but as time went on, his spending grew more careful. (It was never exactly thrifty. Though he was frugal in most other areas, he never stinted on wine, books, or his children.) Sometimes he bought cases, but often he bought single bottles to sample before he invested in larger quantities. Château Cantenac Brown '28 ($1.45) was "lovely; + will develop; buy." Château Beychevelle '34 ($.98) was "a buy," as was Château Pape Clément '34 (also $.98). He complained when he overspent. A Margaux '34 was "Good—not worth $5.39." A Richebourg '37 ($6.95) was "perfect, but the price!" He exulted when he underspent. Château Canon '26 (one case, $18) and Aÿ Brut champagne '28 (four cases, for a New Year's party, each $42) were both a "bargain at the price."

Nine tenths of the wines in the Cellar Book were French. A handful were German. From Spain, only sherries, Montillas, and Riojas; from Portugal, only ports, including one from 1891, the oldest bottle my father bought—*sans nom*, just like the port at Kim's birthday. Italy didn't exist. Australia and Chile and South Africa didn't exist. America didn't exist; Prohibition, which had been repealed less than two years before he bought that case of Clos des Lambrays, had seen to that. I was reading the account of a lost world, written in a dead language. My father's Cellar Book was a record of the time before a case of *Premier Cru* Bordeaux cost as much as a used car. Before cryo-extraction, micro-oxygenation, electrodialysis, inert gas streaming, reverse osmosis, and cross-flow filtration. Before Robert Parker, the wine critic whose hundred-point rating system popularized thick, inky wines with lots of fruit, lots of oak, and lots of alcohol. Before the introduction of three-dollar wines from California's Central Valley, some of whose vineyards yield twelve tons of grapes an acre, as compared with four tons in the Napa Valley and just over two tons in the greatest vineyards of Burgundy and Bordeaux. Before the rise of low-acid, low-tannin wines that are ready to drink immediately—in fact, that *must* be drunk immediately, because if you waited for decades they'd taste like something poured from a fish tank. Before the United States surpassed France as the largest consumer of wine (in volume, not per capita). Before twist-off caps.

The Cellar Book was also a record of my father's life. On October 18, 1935, when he started collecting wine, the Depression had not yet ended, but the economy was improving. During its leanest years, Simon & Schuster, which he had left six months earlier, had cut his salary from one hundred to eighty dollars a week. He was now two years into his tenure at *The New Yorker*. It must have been thrilling to realize that he could afford to hang the expense. He was thirty-one: poignantly young. His marriage to Polly was still happy; Jono was three; for both him and the country, it was a time of gathering optimism.

On the first page of the Cellar Book, he noted that he both bought and stored the wines (what Manhattan apartment would have space for nine hundred and eight bottles?) at "B+S": Bates and Schoonmaker, the wine-importing firm co-owned by Frank Schoonmaker, who advised him on his purchases and made plenty of money in the process. On May 15, 1937, which, of course, I recognized as my father's thirty-third birthday, "B+S" was replaced by "Sherry": Sherry Wine and Spirits (later Sherry-Lehmann), the wine shop that Sam Aaron and his brother had taken over in 1934 from a Prohibition-era bootlegger. Sam had entered his life.

Another big day was October 1, 1938, when he bought fifty-six bottles. October again, just like his first splurge. Autumn was his favorite time of year. To nature lovers, the season of new beginnings is the spring, but to people who excel in school, it's the fall. That fall my father felt flush, because he was four months into his job as emcee of *Information Please*, making $150 a broadcast, with the promise of $250 as soon as the show was commercially sponsored. (Canada Dry signed up the next month. By the early 1940s, when the sponsor was the American Tobacco Company, he was making $1,500.)

There was a gap in the Cellar Book between 1943 and 1948. His first marriage was falling apart.

Then, on October 1, 1948—true to his calendrical pattern—he had another big day. Not only did he buy eighty-seven bottles (from Sam), but they were all magnificent: one case each of Lafite Rothschild, Margaux, Mouton Rothschild, and Haut-Brion, all '45; two cases of Volnay Clos des Ducs '43; and three bottles of Clos de Vougeot '43. He had met my mother.

In June, July, and August of 1950, he noted—under the heading "<u>We drank:</u>"—thirteen wines, almost all of them half bottles, a mix of red and white, grand and modest. My parents had married in February, and my father was teaching my mother about wine, being careful neither to press large quantities on her nor to assume she would prefer a Margaux to a Pouilly-Fuissé.

The last entry in the Cellar Book—a case of Poret Corton '37—was dated October 3, 1950. My mother had just found out she was pregnant. On this go-round he had resolved to be a more attentive husband and father. He might have felt guilty if my mother had caught him fussily transcribing prices and writing "Quite pleasant but overpriced."

The Cellar Book was a book with one reader. My

father had written it; I was the only person who had ever read it. I was the only person who *could* read it. It was like a coded manuscript. I knew that B+S meant Bates and Schoonmaker. I knew the chronology of my father's career and his personal milestones. I knew that all his life he preferred Bordeaux to Burgundies. I knew why the dollar signs mattered so much. I knew that some of the wines he tasted here, perhaps for the first time, returned at the most significant moments of his life: Latour at Kim's twenty-first birthday party, Lafite Rothschild at his own eightieth. I could decipher his handwriting.

"I turn the pages of my Cellar Book," he had written in the last paragraph of "Brief History of a Love Affair." And that's when he'd quoted T. S. Eliot: *These fragments I have shored against my ruins.*

These really *were* fragments: a jumble of torn, mismatched pages. But the Cellar Book was the least fragmentary thing he wrote. Many of his books went unfinished, but not this one. It had a beginning, a middle, and an end. A whole book. The most serious book he ever wrote, the most heartfelt, the most honest. His other writing often buried what he most valued under layers of wit and irony and self-deprecation, but this did not.

My father enjoyed arranging books on his shelves and wines in their racks. "Merely to shelve a new book properly is pleasurable," he wrote, "as filling a vacant space is. Similarly, to bin a case of wine—always alone, this is not a social pleasure—never fails to induce in me a succession of pleasurable thoughts, daydreams, images. A wine cellar, even one as small as mine, has a monastic quality;

the fever and fret of the outside world can never penetrate to these tranquil life essences, living their careers of
growing perfection behind translucent glass." He liked
thinking about a bottle waiting for decades in a hushed,
dark place until a hand reached in, and the corkscrew did
its work, and the wine came to life again, a life that had
deepened while it bided its time. Opening the Cellar Book
was like that.

My father stopped recording the wines he bought in
1950, but he did not stop drinking them. The WINE
MEMORABILIA folder contained a list of the wines from
his own cellar that he served on May 15, 1953—his forty-
ninth birthday—at a small private dinner he and my
mother hosted at a ritzy French restaurant called Maud
Chez Elle. Their guests were the journalist Alistair Cooke
and the publisher Donald Klopfer, who were named on
the menu, and their wives, who weren't. I thought that
disgraceful until I remembered that at fifteen I'd addressed
those letters from France to The Clifton Fadimans.

The wine list was a rough draft in my father's handwriting. The blue-gray ink was fading, and the vintage of
the champagne, a Moët et Chandon Cuvée Dom Pérignon, was hidden behind discolored tape. I was im-
pressed by the geographic range of the wines: three
French; one German, a Piesporter Goldtröpfchen feinste
Auslese '49; and one Hungarian, the dessert wine, an
1876 Tokay. (Like fortified wines, sweet wines can have
very long lives.) I found out later that the Bonnes Mares
'23—a magnum—was the first-string choice to accompany the entrée, to be replaced by the alternate only if it

Moët et Chandon Cuvée Dom Perignon 19

Piesporter Goldtröpfchen feinste Auslese
Fuder Nr 9110, Flasche
Nr 174, Original - Abfüllung
Reichsgraf von Kesselstatt,
Bundes Siegerpreis, 1949

—

Les Bonnes Mares, 1923
or
La Romanée Conti, 1923

—

Tokayer Ausbruch, 1876
so

May 15, 1953,   Maud Chez Elle

The Maud Chez Elle wine list, 1953

hadn't held up. It had. I wish it had proved unworthy. My mother was six months pregnant with me at the time, and in that casual obstetric era I doubt that she was discouraged from drinking wine. Bonnes Mares is a fine Burgundy, but I would have enjoyed thinking that I spent three months floating in amniotic fluid composed partly of the backup wine, Romanée-Conti '33.

Tucked behind the wine list was a menu tied with a tasseled crimson cord. It must have been printed on very high-quality stock, since it was the only document in the WINE MEMORABILIA folder that wasn't falling apart. The date was September 10, 1959. The venue was the "21" Club, a celebrity hangout that during its speakeasy days had hidden its wine in the cellar of the building next door, number 19, thus allowing its employees to deny truthfully that there was liquor on the premises. It had also been the venue of the 1958 Cigar Institute of America Ladies' Smoker, at which my father had asserted that women were bad at conversation and knew nothing about wine. This, by contrast, was to be an all-male occasion, to which he invited six colleagues to celebrate his eighth anniversary as a columnist for *Holiday* magazine. It seemed to me that *Holiday* should have thrown the dinner for *him*, but perhaps it was better this way; if he'd been a guest, my father couldn't have chosen the menu, which included eight courses and five wines, not to mention aperitifs, cocktails, and spirits.

Like the menu I'd calligraphed for Kim's birthday, this one might have benefited from some proofreading (a compulsion in which my father and I both indulged

Aperitifs et Cocktails

"Hope" Madeira
Cellers of E. T. Gerry 1835

Schloss Johannisberger
Auslese 1949 Fass Nr 67

Magnum
Hospices de Beaune 1947

Hooper's Vintage Port 1920
Magnum Bollinger Brut 1949

Marc de Bourgogne
(Marc de Vignoble de Meursault)

Menu

Le Saumon de Terre Neuve Fumé
L'Esturgeon du Lac

L'Essence de Queue de Boeuf
Celeri et Olives

Le Filet de Sole Anglaise Marguery

Le Coq de Bruyère Rôti sur Canapé
Le Celeri Braisé
Le Riz Sauvage

Le Sorbet de Limon, Menthe Verte

Les Fromages: Bel Paese, Brie, Stilton
Le Crêpe Soufflé "21"

Café des Princes

Hine Grande Fine Champagne
Ballantine's Scotch Liqueur
Cigars "21" Cabinet Selection
Cigarets

Maître de
Cuisine.
Yves L. Ploneis

The "21" Club menu, 1959

reflexively and enjoyably, though he with greater skill). Whoever wrote it had drawn the accent over "Café" at the wrong angle and left the accents entirely off "Céleri," "Rôti," "Canapé," "Crêpe," and "Maître." "Le Sorbet de Limon" was an unorthodox palate-cleanser, since in French "limon" means neither lemon nor lime; the diners had apparently been served Silt Sherbet. On the wine list, "Cellars" was misspelled. . . .

Wait a second.

"Cellers of E. T. Gerry 1835."

And on the line above it, " 'Hope' Madeira."

Oh my God, there's my Madeira!

My father drank it with his oxtail soup.

I felt dizzy. I'd never thought about the contents of my bottle being consumed at a particular time or in a particular place. I'd never even pictured it having once been full. As I stared at the menu, my Madeira bottle, with its tobacco-colored pattern of sediment, sat on a shelf not ten feet away. I kept looking at the menu, and then at the bottle, and then at the menu and the bottle and the menu and the bottle.

The WINE MEMORABILIA folder contained one more item: "Remembrance of Drinks Past," an article torn out of *GQ*. He had written it when he was eighty. I had never read it. A slightly different version, under a different title, was included in *The New Joys of Wine*, but although I had read the original *Joys of Wine* from cover to cover, I had assumed the later edition contained a few updates of interest only to—well, to people who really liked wine, and I'd stowed it under my bed, on top of its predecessor, since I had no shelf tall enough to accommodate them. "Remembrance of Drinks Past" recalled a quartet of what my father called "wine epiphanies." The wines were the white Graves in Paris, the 1927 Cockburn port that had lifted his depression, the La Tâche '49 he and my mother had drunk with Mortimer Adler, and the wines served at the dinner at "21." Why did he keep the article in the folder after it had been published in a book? Not for himself. For the person who would find the menu from "21" after he was no longer around to explain it. It was like accompanying a photograph with a caption.

"I admit that I went all out," wrote my father, "withdrawing from my modest"—yeah, right—"cellar the very finest wines I owned. The food was first-rate, but no Filet of Sole Marguery or Coq de Bruyère *rôti sur canapé*, even if superb, has the power to illuminate the memory twenty-five years afterward. Wine has." *He* got all the accents right.

There was a description of the wine served with every course. For instance: "With the grouse was presented a magnum of Hospices de Beaune '47—I think an Aloxe-Corton." The assumption was that the reader, who of course was male and almost certainly not from Brooklyn, was on cozy terms with each part of that sentence: not only was he accustomed to eating grouse, but he knew that a magnum was a big bottle; that Hospices de Beaune was a fine Burgundy *domaine* whose annual charity auction was an important event in the wine world; and that (but of course!) Aloxe-Corton, home to some of the Hospices vineyards, was a *commune* that produced the best reds in the Côte de Beaune.

Of my Madeira, my father wrote, "Though frail, it was still living at age 124, but you had to give it your close attention. It could sing only at piccolo pitch. Still, the notes were true."

"Still, the notes were true." Reading those words fifty years after he met the singer, I could tell how happy he had been when he wrote them. When he looked at the menu as an old man, it brought back everything: the food, the wine, the private dining room, the pride he took in being able to pay for such a dinner, the convergence of his life as a writer and his life as an oenophile, the conviviality that grew as the night continued and everyone had a little too much to drink but not enough to impair the quality of the conversation, some of which, I feel sure, was about the wines themselves.

My father may have felt like an outsider in many aspects of his life, but when he drank wine with friends, he always belonged. Unless he was with Frank Schoonmaker or Sam Aaron, he knew more about it than anyone else in the room. He was confident and playful and at ease with himself, the way one might be in the presence of a lover. As he had once written in a letter to an old friend, he never felt counterfeit when he was in love. He was in love with wine.

The folder seemed to glow with joy, as if the memory of my father's pleasure was so strong as to render it faintly radioactive. Just as the menu had brought back the dinner at "21" to him, WINE MEMORABILIA brought him back to me. He occasionally appeared in my dreams, and they always made me glad, because they were the only time I got to see him. This felt something like that. As I stood in my study on that summer night, bending over the *Encyclopædia Britannica* bookcase, I remembered him more vividly than I had at any moment since his death.

23

Port

I learned that my father had cancer in October of 1998. He was ninety-four. Everything had been in readiness for years. Living Will. Durable Power of Attorney. DNR order. In Case of Death instructions (with revisions dictated frequently to his secretary and distributed to his family, each time with the directive to "Destroy All Previous Versions," one iteration of which contained the sentence "As I have never died before, I do not know how the survivor manages these inevitable details"). Address and phone number of the Harvey-Engelhardt Funeral Home and Crematory in Fort Myers, at which we were enjoined to purchase the cheapest possible cremation and ask Mr. Harvey and Mr. Engelhardt to discard the ashes. What could be more gratifying for a man who liked to throw things out than to be thrown out himself? (In the event, I disobeyed him and, with Jono and his wife, Mary Lou, scattered some of the ashes on a few carefully chosen graves in their hometown of Concord, Massachusetts. This was almost certainly illegal, but it was nice to know that a few Fadiman molecules were in close proximity to those of Emerson, Thoreau, Hawthorne, and Bronson Alcott.)

My father's attitudes were also in readiness. For twenty-five years he had been copying stoic passages about death into his *Worth a Jot* journals and, after he lost his sight, scrawling summaries on Maxi-Aids pads. Homer on how a generation of men is like a generation of leaves that must fall so that new plants may grow. Socrates on the virtue of making one's end in a tranquil frame of mind. Chuang-Tzu on how birth and death are like the rotation of the seasons. His favorite: George Bernard Shaw on the joy of being thoroughly worn out before you are thrown on the scrap heap.

Everything was in readiness, that is to say, except my father. Six years earlier he had been ready to commit suicide, but now nothing could have been further from his mind. There was simply too much enjoyment to be extracted from listening to books, reciting nonsense rhymes to Susannah and Henry, and drinking wine, about which he had once written, "Yes, we have had our ups and downs, wine and I, our misunderstandings and our reconciliations, our delights and our discords. On the whole, however, I think of ourselves as a model couple: faithful, mutually solicitous, still ardent, and, in the case of the lady, well preserved." More than four decades had passed since he wrote those words. They were still true.

I wasn't ready either. When my mother called to say he had jaundice and might have pancreatic cancer, which

With Susannah, six months
before his death, 1998

indeed turned out to be the case, I was taken completely by surprise. He had lived so far beyond any reasonable expectation, rising Phoenix-like from the ashes of his blindness, that on some level I thought he was immortal. What did I expect? Not death. Nor would I have expected it if he'd been 104. In fact, part of me still believes that if he hadn't gotten cancer, he'd be alive today at age 113, like a Russian Methuselah from a yogurt commercial, waiting for the next Talking Book to arrive.

He defied expectations again. We were told he'd be dead in three months, but he lasted for eight. I flew down from New York for three days every three weeks. Kim resigned from his several jobs in Wyoming and rented a cottage on Sanibel, ten minutes from our parents. Instead of sending cassettes, he read Book-of-the-Month Club manuscripts to our father in person and took down his dictated notes, one of the last of which, on a mediocre crime novel, contained the sentences "As a thriller it does not thrill. As a chiller it does not chill."

During the first three months, our father could still eat out at restaurants. Then he fell, and our mother knew she could no longer take care of him. She was sick too, though she hadn't found out yet; after his death she would be diagnosed with Parkinson's disease and end-stage breast cancer, and would outlive him by only two and a half years.

The day after my father's fall, she and Kim drove him to a nursing home, took one look, turned around, rented a hospital bed, and moved him into Kim's cottage. First he couldn't walk, then he couldn't stand, then he couldn't bathe himself, then he had a series of transient ischemic strokes that robbed him of some easy words. One afternoon he couldn't remember "carrot." But on another, after I told him about an essay I was planning to write about Samuel Taylor Coleridge, and I thought he was asleep, he murmured, "Silas Tomkyn Comberbache": the alias Coleridge used when he ran away from Cambridge and enlisted in the 15th Light Dragoons. And one night, seemingly apropos of nothing, he said, "Sleep after toil, port after stormy seas." Only after I found the wine folder and read "Remembrance of Drinks Past" did I understand that this was a line from *The Faerie Queene*. He'd quoted it when he described the 1927 Cockburn port that, on a stormy winter night, had offered him the consolation he badly needed. In his article, the double meaning of "port" was a witticism—a wine pun—but this time, in his last weeks, he had a different kind of port in mind. He must have been thinking of the line that followed: "Ease after war, death after life, does greatly please." He was finally approaching readiness.

Whenever I left to fly back to my family, his last word, as it had always been, was "Blessings."

On his ninety-fifth birthday, sitting next to a window with a view of palmettos and bougainvillea (not that he could see them), we ate Nova and sturgeon I had ordered from a New York delicatessen. After a lifetime of pushing Jewish food away, he craved it. It was as if he'd crossed the river in the other direction and was coming home to Brooklyn.

Brillat-Savarin wrote that when his beloved great-aunt was dying, he told her it would do her good to drink some fine wine. She gratefully swallowed half a glass of the best his cellar had to offer, instantly grew stronger, uttered some suspiciously articulate last words, and expired. My father wasn't so fortunate. He had once written that the palate was one of the last of the organs to decay. True, perhaps, but eventually the cancer trashed his sense of taste. He lost his desire for wine. It just didn't taste right. The only drink he wanted was Guinness, which, he told Kim, "tastes like *something*." His appetite evaporated when he saw too large a plate, too full a glass. He asked Kim to pour an ounce at a time, fifteen times a day.

Every hour he was more worn out and ready for the scrap heap, in proper Shaw fashion, though Shaw had died at only ninety-four and my father went him one year better. Visiting nurses came, and he talked with them late into the night, just as he had in his room on the eighth floor of Mount Sinai Hospital. Kim cooked for him, changed his sheets, carried him to the bathroom, occasionally bathed him, and gave him eleven different kinds of pills each day. The physical care was harder for Kim than it was for me when I spelled him, perhaps because he'd never taken care of babies. Not that our father looked anything like a baby. He had always been mildly pudgy but now weighed less than a hundred pounds. His skin was translucent, and his back was covered with skin tags and cherry angiomas and iffy-looking moles of the kind you might have wanted a dermatologist to take a look at if the patient hadn't been about to die of something else.

I flew in from New York on my father's last night. He was unconscious and breathing loudly and irregularly. I climbed into his hospital bed. It was the second time in my life that we'd spent the night in the same room. His breaths became less labored as soon as I lay down next to him: the sort of thing I'd read about but never put any stock in, because Fadimans, as you know, are a rational, secular bunch.

The next morning, I walked out to the living room to talk to Kim. My father chose to die in that ten-minute window of privacy, as if not to be bothersome or over-dramatic. It was Father's Day.

It is not true that people become something other than themselves as soon as they die. I kissed his forehead. I talked to him for a while even though I knew he couldn't hear me. I told him what a good father he had been and that I loved him. I thanked him.

Ten years later, I found the Cellar Book. He left me his papers and he knew I'd find it.

The first sentence of "Brief History of a Love Affair," which he wrote when he was younger than I am now, is "Like most love stories, mine will mean something to lovers; rather less to those merely capable of love; to the incapable, nothing."

That turned out not to be true. It did mean something to me.

Notes on Sources

Any memoir, especially one dealing with events that took place both before and after the author was born, relies on a mixture of personal and public sources.

The essential grist was my memories of the just-under-forty-six years that my life overlapped with my father's, along with the eighteen years I've spent since then continuing to try to figure him out. Memories are fallible, so I cross-checked them as much as possible with my brother Kim, who enriched the book with many of his own. I also looked through dozens of boxes of memory-triggering family photographs.

As my father's literary executor, I had access to all his files, which included, among many other things, the résumé on which he listed his hobbies as wine and the avoidance of exercise; his excessively complete medical records; his "In Case of Death" documents; and his WINE MEMORABILIA folder. His files also contained the letters he had received from dozens of writers, copies of a handful he wrote himself, and all the letters I had ever sent him, including those from my homesick summer in France in 1969. I also kept all the letters he sent *me* in France, in addition to hundreds he wrote to me over the next three decades. My mother saved many of his letters as well, including those he wrote to her nearly every day, both on board the RMS *Queen Elizabeth* and in England, during his month-long reporting assignment for *Holiday* magazine in 1958.

I could not have written this book without the 194-page transcript of a series of taped conversations I had with my father in New York and Santa Barbara, ostensibly in preparation for "Clifton Fadiman at Eighty," the article for *Life* (October 1984). My editors knew that the piece hardly required such exhaustive research and that most of the material would never make it in. (Magazines could afford to be more generous in those days. Thanks, *Life*.) This book contains no reconstructed or imagined quotations. When my father told me, apropos of his trip to Paris to retrieve his first wife, "There was nothing else to do but eat and practice our French and screw," I recorded it; when he registered his horror of the lettuce garnish at the Quilted Giraffe, I wrote it down; when he smoked a panatela while showing me his wine closet, his cigar-muffled intonations were preserved on tape. The article itself also provided much useful material.

Which brings me to the topic of writing about events one has written about before. When I began this project, I thought that if I had mentioned an incident in *Life*, however briefly, or in one of my later essays (for instance, my lunch at La Pyramide or my father's attempt to reconstruct the Milton sonnet at the Bascom Palmer Eye Institute), it had to be retired forever, even if I wished to tell it differently or at greater length. My family eventually convinced me that this was a bad idea—that this book was *the* thing I was going to write about my father, and leaving out anything good would be foolish.

All extended quotations not from written sources are quoted verbatim or close to verbatim from those 1984 conversations; from notes I took, mostly in 1993, after my father lost his sight (I thought that I might want to write about his blindness someday or that the notes might prove useful for an essay of his own); and from the transcript of two marvelous conversations he had with the literary critic Diana Trilling, a close friend for more than half a century, mostly about Columbia in the 1920s but also about his childhood and his early career, recorded for the Columbia Center for Oral History Archives at the Rare Book and Manuscript Library on April 21 and June 7, 1976.

The heart of this book is my father's writing. Almost all his books are out of print, so I derived enormous pleasure from the prospect of sharing (one of his least favorite gerunds) his witty, articulate voice with readers who might not otherwise have the chance to hear it. His work also provided useful background information and occasionally, by some form of associative sorcery akin to that worked by the old photographs, stirred long-buried memories. I drew on his three essay collections, *Party of One*, *Any Number Can Play*, and *Enter, Conversing*; the introductions to two of his anthologies, *Reading I've Liked* ("My Life Is an Open Book: Confessions and Digressions of an Incurable," the essay that made Carolyn Heilbrun vow to become "a Fadiman") and *Party of Twenty*; both *The Lifetime Reading Plan*, which guided readers through a hundred Great Books, almost all by dead white males, and *The New Lifetime Reading Plan*, co-authored with John S. Major, which substantially broadened the list; *The World Treasury of Children's Literature* (he never finished his critical history on the subject, but he published a dandy three-volume anthology of his favorite gleanings from his years of research); two collections he edited in his late eighties and nineties, *The Treasury of the Encyclopædia Britannica* and (with co-editors Katharine Washburn and John S. Major) *World Poetry: An Anthology of Verse from Antiquity to Our Time*; and "To the Curious, Intelligent Reader," a booklet-sized reprint of his remarks on accepting the National Book Award for Distinguished Contribution to American Letters. I cannot omit mention of *Wally the Wordworm*, the children's book, based on stories our father told to Kim and me, about the bookworm who ate his way through a dictionary. If you can find it, I recommend the original edition, illustrated by Arnold Roth, in which Wally wears a red baseball cap, rather than the later (and, in our family's view, inferior) edition in which he wears a far-too-fancy yellow top hat and also, strangely, resembles a sperm. A Bede

Productions audiocassette of my father reading the book aloud is occasionally available from used-book sites.

I also made use of my father's unpublished work: the manuscript of *Worth a Jot*, the compilation of journal entries he wrote in his eighties; the also-ran entries; and the notes he made when he was blind—some dictated to his secretary and some written in Magic Marker on Maxi-Aids pads—for his unfinished book *When I Consider*.

One of my most crucial sources was, of course, my father's wine writing. *The New Joys of Wine*—the revised, souped-up descendant of the original *Joys of Wine*, both co-authored with Sam Aaron—was open on my desk (leaving little room for anything else) during much of the time I worked on this book. I turned to it for information, for images so ravishing they temporarily made me forget I didn't love wine, and for three of my father's wine essays: the oft-quoted "Brief History of a Love Affair" (which originally appeared in *Holiday*, then in *Any Number Can Play*); "Seventeen Years Later"; and "Four Wine Epiphanies" (which originally appeared in *GQ*, under the title "Remembrance of Drinks Past"). *Wine Buyers Guide*, another Fadiman-Aaron production, gave me a sense of the wine world of the mid-1970s. I also drew on my father's introduction to *Dionysus: A Case of Vintage Tales about Wine,* in which, among other things, he described the birthday dinner at Maud Chez Elle whose wine list I found in the WINE MEMORABILIA folder.

From this point on, I will note sources by topic. This isn't an exhaustive list. I've included only the works that were most helpful to me or potentially most interesting to readers. On occasion I've mentioned a discrepancy between accounts.

On wine: Among the books I inherited from my father, my favorites were *Notes on a Cellar-Book*, by George Saintsbury (my father once wrote that it would still be read when all the author's scholarship had turned to dust, though he later reassessed it with less enthusiasm); *The Story of Wine*, by Hugh Johnson; *The Great Wines of Europe*, by Ernst Hornickel; *The Signet Book of Wine*, by

Alexis Bespaloff; and the *Encyclopædia of Wines and Spirits*, by Alexis Lichine, which I always liked opening because of its lavish inscription to my father. I enjoyed *The Complete Wine Book*, by Frank Schoonmaker and Tom Marvel, which my father published at Simon & Schuster soon after the end of Prohibition, though I had to buy a copy myself, since he'd kept only the pages he used as his first Cellar Book and, characteristically, thrown out the rest. Among more recent works, *The Wine Bible*, by Karen MacNeil, and *The Science of Wine*, by Jamie Goode, were particularly useful.

On Roald Dahl: "Taste," the story that fascinated me in the fifth grade, was from Dahl's collection *Someone Like You*. The tan-and-lavender edition I originally read in the early sixties was also among the books I inherited from my father. "Taste" is reprinted in *Dionysus* and both editions of *The Joys of Wine*.

On my father's family: The spellings of my grandparents' first names, like many names transliterated from Russian, differ in various sources. I've used "Isadore" because that's how it appeared in the U.S. Federal Census for many decades, starting in 1900, as well as in Social Security and draft registration records, though elsewhere I've found "Isidore" and "Isidor." The spelling of my grandmother's original first name is even harder to pin down, because she called herself Grace for most of her adult life. The most reliable source available is the State of New York record of her 1898 marriage, which she signed "Bettemi," though I've seen "Betteni" in other sources. She was also sometimes called Bessie.

On my father's childhood: "A Note on a Brooklyn Drugstore Childhood" (in *Enter, Conversing*) provided useful details. The early achievements of my father and his formidable elder brother, Ed, came from 1916 and 1920 editions of the Boys High School *Recorder*, as well as from the *Brooklyn Daily Eagle* and the *Brooklyn Standard Union*. An amusing discrepancy between accounts of my father's first encounter with alcohol: In "Brief History of a Love Affair," he wrote that when he was "about eleven," he drank an excess of *kümmel* at "the house of a family friend." When he told me about the incident, he said he was about fourteen—

a likelier age, given that the "family friend" was actually Ed, whom he presumably wished to protect from accusations of child endangerment.

On my father's experience as an undergraduate at Columbia: I learned a great deal from Diana Trilling's memoir, *The Beginning of the Journey*, which also discussed my father's relationship with her husband, Lionel Trilling. *Whittaker Chambers: A Biography*, by Sam Tanenhaus, and *Cold Friday*, by Whittaker Chambers, described my father's circle of friends. The *Columbia Daily Spectator* and *The Columbian* provided a useful picture of student life. Tuition and room fees were from the *Columbia University Bulletin of Information: Columbia College Announcement 1922–1923*: midway through his time at college. I read about John Erskine's General Honors course in *An Oasis of Order: The Core Curriculum at Columbia College*, by Timothy P. Cross, and in Erskine's own *My Life as a Teacher*.

On my father's early political leanings: Although it would be exciting if I could report that he was once a Communist, he wasn't. Before and during the McCarthy era, he was frequently attacked by the right-wing journalist Westbrook Pegler, who, as my father put it, "wanted to ruin me." Pegler referred repeatedly to an article my father had contributed to a September 1932 symposium in the *New Masses*, an American Marxist magazine, called "How I Came to Communism." What Pegler didn't mention was that (along with Sherwood Anderson, Upton Sinclair, and Granville Hicks, among others) my father had been invited to write about why he had turned left, not why he had become a Communist. As a favor to his old classmate Whittaker Chambers, a member of the magazine's editorial board, he had done so. "The Menorah Group Moves Left," by Alan M. Wald (*Jewish Social Studies*, Summer–Autumn 1976), quotes Felix Morrow as recalling, "Poor Fadiman! This was not his title, nor does the article say more than he is moving leftward." Chambers apparently changed the title of the symposium "as a funny practical joke."

On Prohibition: I relied on *Last Call: The Rise and Fall of Pro-*

hibition, Daniel Okrent's sprightly history. The list of synonyms for "drunk" came from *The American Earthquake*, by Edmund Wilson.

On my father's early career: Two particularly useful contemporary accounts were a 1942 profile by John Chamberlain called "Fadiman for the Millions," in *Post Biographies of Famous Journalists*, and a reporter's file I obtained from the *Time* morgue that formed the basis for "Fadiman Quits" (*Time*, September 27, 1943), on why my father left *The New Yorker*. Much of my material on *Information Please* came from *Information, Please!*, by Dan Golenpaul; *Information, Please*, by Martin Grams, Jr.; and *Quiz Craze*, by Thomas A. DeLong.

On my father's views on women: Carolyn Heilbrun's *When Men Were the Only Models We Had* contained discomfiting but important insights. Heilbrun was also a shrewd commentator on academic life at Columbia. When I finished her book, I couldn't wait to talk with her about my father; I don't remember ever having been more disappointed to learn that an author I'd presumed living had already died.

On my mother: If any readers find themselves curious about my mother, Annalee Whitmore Jacoby Fadiman, they might wish to read *They Call It Pacific*, by Clark Lee; *China Reporting*, by Stephen R. MacKinnon and Oris Friesen; *China Hands*, by Peter Rand; *The Women Who Wrote the War*, by Nancy Caldwell Sorel; or *Eve of a Hundred Midnights*, by Bill Lascher, a suspenseful account of her wartime marriage to, and escape from Corregidor with, her first husband, Melville Jacoby.

On Jewish college admissions: Theodore H. White's *In Search of History* contained the taxonomy of students as white men, gray men, and meatballs. Columbia's admissions policies were detailed in Harold S. Wechsler's clear and comprehensive history *The Qualified Student*, as well as in his article "The Rationale for Ethnicity: Ethnicity and College Admission in America, 1910–1980" (*American Quarterly*, Winter 1984); *The Chosen*, by Jerome Karabel; *Stand, Columbia*, by Robert McCaughey; *Jews in the Academy*,

1900–1940, by Susanne Klingenstein; and "How Jewish Quotas Began," by Stephen Steinberg (*Commentary*, September 1, 1971). Contemporary sources included *Columbia*, by Frederick Paul Keppel, the second dean of Columbia College; "May Jews Go to College?" (*The Nation*, June 14, 1922); Columbia University's *Annual Report of the President and Treasurer to the Trustees with Accompanying Documents for the Year Ending June 30, 1919*, and similar reports for 1920 and 1921; "The Spirit of Morningside: Some Notes on Columbia University," by M. G. Torch, described in the contributors' list as "the pseudonym of a young graduate of Columbia University" (*The Menorah Journal*, March 1930); and (a document for which I am indebted to the late Harold Wechsler) a June 9, 1922, letter from Herbert E. Hawkes, the third dean of Columbia College, to Professor Edmund Beecher Wilson, about Columbia's policy of trying to "eliminate the low grade boy," who, he explained, often happened to be an over-ambitious New York City Jew.

On anti-Semitism in the academy: My understanding was deepened by *New York Jew,* by Alfred Kazin; by "America Is Home," by Nathan Abrams, in Commentary *in American Life*, edited by Murray Friedman; and by an April 1, 1986, letter to *Commentary* by Estelle Gilson that mentions Morris Raphael Cohen, the philosopher who did not know how to wear a dinner jacket. I was fascinated by the awkwardly adulatory tone and the publishing venue (unusual territory for a gentile) of Mark Van Doren's "Jewish Students I Have Known" (*The Menorah Journal*, June 1927), an article that was said to have given him a reputation for "philo-Semitism"; only someone who was accustomed to hearing contemptuous remarks about Jewish students would have felt the need to overcompensate so strenuously.

On middlebrow culture: "The Tenth Muse" (*Harper's Magazine*, September 2001; reprinted in *Concepts of Culture*, edited by Adam Muller), by Jacques Barzun, presented my father as an intellectual leader who had helped civilize the American public. The theme of transmission was emphasized in "A Carrier of Ideas: An

Interview with Clifton Fadiman" (*The Center Magazine*, July/August 1977) and in "Clifton Fadiman '25: An Erudite Guide to the Wisdom of Others" (my father's obituary in *Columbia College Today*, September 1999), a title to which Barzun took exception, because it "ignores the wisdom needed for unerring guidance." In "Masscult and Midcult" (*Partisan Review*, Spring 1960; reprinted in Macdonald's *Masscult and Midcult: Essays Against the American Grain*), Dwight Macdonald included my father among the Midcult popularizers who corrupted and marketed High Culture. As far as I know, Macdonald never called my father "the standard-bearer of middle-brow culture" (as Barzun said he did) or "the high priest of midcult" (as Heilbrun said he did; that phrase was in fact from a summary of Macdonald's views in my father's *New York Times* obituary), but I have little doubt that he would have concurred with those assessments, since in a 1968 interview with *Book World* he crowned my father one of the "kings of the middlebrows" (*Interviews with Dwight Macdonald*, edited by Michael Wreszin).

On Brillat-Savarin: The quotations from Jean Anthelme Brillat-Savarin's *The Physiology of Taste* are all from the edition gorgeously translated and annotated by my father's friend M.F.K. Fisher, the great food writer and certifiable gourmand (she even looked like us). After my father's death, I found eighteen letters from her in his files, one of which said, "By now it seems plain that you are the only person in the world who has read anything I've written in the way I most hoped for."

On Hemingway: The history of what my father called "the letter Hemingway wrote me when he was drunk" merits some explication. The letter was written in response to "A Letter to Mr. Hemingway," my father's review of *Winner Take Nothing* (*The New Yorker*, October 28, 1933). My father often said that because it had arrived years before he realized such letters might be valuable, he'd thrown it out. His secretary, Bert Hunt, remembered the story differently. In a letter to the Hemingway biographer Carlos Baker, she said she'd put it in a folder called IMPORTANT LETTERS TO KEEP (and that my father told her he'd probably tossed out later, when he moved his office) but typed a copy for herself because she wanted to reread it. I'd often heard about the letter but read it for the first time after I met Paul Hendrickson, the author of *Hemingway's Boat*, a fascinating account of the last half of Hemingway's life. Hendrickson mentioned the letter, sent me part of it, and directed me to the Carlos Baker Collection of Ernest Hemingway in the Princeton University Library, where Bert Hunt's copy is archived. Hendrickson wrote in his book that the original "may have been typed," but in her 1976 conversation with my father, Diana Trilling described the letter—which she and Lionel had seen before it disappeared—as handwritten, "all the way through the margins, up and down, around." Incidentally, Hemingway wasn't entirely joking when he invited my father to watch him "break Max Eastman's jaw." Four years after Eastman wrote a review called "Bull in the Afternoon" (*The New Republic*, June 7, 1933), in which he compared Hemingway's literary style to "wearing false hair on the chest," Hemingway met him by chance in the office of their editor, Max Perkins; unbuttoned both his shirt and Eastman's in order to reveal the abundance of his own (real) chest hair and Eastman's relative paucity; hit Eastman in the face with *Art and the Life of Action*, a book that contained the review; broke the book's spine, though not Eastman's jaw; and wrestled with Eastman until Perkins intervened. Unfortunately, my father was not there to watch.

On Sidney Franklin: The "Brooklyn Bullfighter" is widely referred to as my father's cousin, but they didn't share grandparents; my father told me Franklin was his second or third cousin. In *Death in the Afternoon*, Hemingway, who knew Franklin well, called him "one of the most skillful, graceful, and slow manipulators of a cape fighting to-day," though his admiration eventually cooled. Franklin's autobiography, *Bullfighter from Brooklyn*, is rollicking, if shamelessly inaccurate. Lillian Ross published a three-part *New Yorker* profile of Franklin, "El Único Matador," in March 1949 (reprinted in Ross's *Reporting* and, in part, in *Reporting Always*). More recently, *Double-Edged Sword*, a biography by Bart Paul, revealed that Franklin was gay, though diligently closeted.

Paul wrote that Sidney's original last name was "Frumpkin," but his niece, DorisAnn Kolodny Markowitz, told me that it never had a *p*; it was "Frumkin," which is how my father (and Ross) spelled it.

On port: In "Seventeen Years Later," my father wrote that during a period of depression, he had drunk "two or three glasses of an inexpensive port" every evening. In "Four Wine Epiphanies," he described drinking a far more expensive port on a single, stormy night, also in the midst of a depression: "Among the few bottles I kept in my office was some vintage port, a wine I love. I may be mistaken, but I decanted what I now think was a Cockburn of that great year 1927." The second account appeared to correct the first, if without absolute certitude, but it's possible that both were true, or that only the first was.

On the Book-of-the-Month Club: I drew on *A Family of Readers*, by William Zinsser; *The Book of the Month*, edited by Al Silverman; *A Feeling for Books*, by Janice A. Radway; "There Goes the Judge," by Wilfrid Sheed (*The Yale Review*, January 1999); my father's reports on manuscripts; and his reviews in the *Book-of-the-Month Club News*.

On VIP: I learned about my father's experience at VIP (now called Lighthouse of Southwest Florida), the vision rehabilitation agency in Fort Myers at which my father took a class in independent living skills, both from the notes I took during our phone calls and from recent interviews with his instructor, Sue Wild.

On taste science: Most of my material came from interviews and correspondence with Virginia Utermohlen, the former director of the Cornell Taste Science Laboratory, and Larry Marks, a fellow at and emeritus director of the John B. Pierce Laboratory at Yale, as well as from correspondence with Barry Green, also a fellow at the Pierce lab. Dr. Utermohlen's website, www.tastescience.com, contained much helpful information. Other useful sources included Dr. Utermohlen's "Was Proust a Taster? Taste Sensitivity to 6-*n*-Propylthiouracil and the Relationships Among Memory, Imagination, Synesthesia, and Emotional Response to Visual Experience"

(*Food and Foodways*, Issue 3, 2002); *Proust Was a Neuroscientist*, by Jonah Lehrer; *The Taste of Sweet*, by Joanne Chen; "The PROP Test and Reactions to It," by Jancis Robinson (www.jancisrobinson.com); "The Gustin (CA6) Gene Polymorphism, rs2274333 (A/G), as a Mechanistic Link Between PROP Tasting and Fungiform Taste Papilla Density and Maintenance," by Melania Melis et al. (*PLOS ONE*, September 2013); "Bitter Receptor Gene (*TAS2R38*), 6-*n*-Propylthiouracil (PROP) Bitterness and Alcohol Intake," by Valerie B. Duffy et al. (*Alcoholism: Clinical and Experimental Research*, November 2004); and my genetic reports and raw data from 23andMe.

Acknowledgments

This book started eight years ago when I suggested a few article ideas to Ben Metcalf, then an editor at *Harper's*. At one point in the conversation, I said, "I think I could tell the story of my father's life and character through wine."

" 'The Oenophile's Daughter!' " he exclaimed.

Ben and *Harper's* parted ways; I realized I needed to write a book, not an article; and the title met its Waterloo after I discovered that hardly anyone knew how to spell, pronounce, or define "oenophile." (I felt better after I was reminded that Nabokov's original title for *Speak, Memory*, perhaps my favorite book, was *Speak, Mnemosyne*. Same problems.) But Ben's three words had set me in motion, both giving me permission to include myself in the narrative and launching me on a long and sometimes circuitous quest for a fuller understanding of my father.

En route to *The Wine Lover's Daughter*, I was lent a hand by many generous people.

My father liked to say that wine was an intelligible field of study. Among those who helped make it more intelligible to me were Ric Hopper, Fred Holley, and Victoria Sadosky. Mannie Berk, the founder of The Rare Wine Co., commented on my father's Cellar Book and shared his extensive knowledge of Madeira. My old friend Sam Perkins, the former executive editor of *Wine Enthusiast*, shed light on many aspects of oenology and oenophilia (*he* knew what it meant). Monique Josse at the Musée du Vin in Paris, Pauline Delmarle at the Musée du Vin et du Négoce in Bordeaux, Jean-Marie Verbrugghe at the Écomusée de la Vigne et du Vin in Gradignan, and Tracey Dello Stritto at the Finger Lakes Wine Alliance responded swiftly and helpfully to wine-related queries. Julia van der Vink, a viticulturist and former sommelier, provided a winemaker's perspective, answered an incessant stream of questions about both French and California wines, and often saved me from embarrassing myself. Over the years, I had many conversations about wine with my friend John Laird and my former literary agent Robert Lescher. I wish they were still alive so we could have more.

I wrote part of *The Wine Lover's Daughter* as a fellow at the MacDowell Colony, than which there could be no more perfect place to write. The book was enriched by conversations about writing, wine, fathers, and Judaism with fellow fellows Alicia Svigals, Stewart Wallace, Maureen McLane, Ruth Franklin, David Petersen, and, especially, Alex Halberstadt.

I am grateful to the Norman Mailer Center for enabling me to write a chapter in the Mailer house in Provincetown, and to Mary Dearborn and Eric Laursen for renting me the phone-less and usually-Internet-less one-room cabin—paradise!—in which I wrote the last half of the book. Conveniently, Mary happened to be the author of the recent and excellent *Ernest Hemingway: A Biography*, so she also served as a valuable Hemingway resource.

Oh, how I love my publisher, Farrar, Straus and Giroux! Who would not feel fortunate to have her book gracefully designed on the inside by Jonathan Lippincott and on the outside by Alex Merto, meticulously (but not officiously) copy-edited by Susan Goldfarb and Lisa Silverman, gently shooed along its editorial path by Carolina Baizan, expertly brought to the attention of its readers by Jeff Seroy and Sarita Varma—and, above all, sensitively edited by Jonathan Galassi, whom I've known for more than forty years but whom I still think of, with awe, as the God of Books?

It was my lucky day when Lynn Nesbit, who (as far as I can see) is both telepathic and omnipotent, became my literary agent: I have only to wish for something and presto!, she has made it happen.

I am grateful to Paul Hendrickson for telling me that Hemingway's memorable letter to my father—or at least a copy of it—had not been lost and for pointing me in its direction; to AnnaLee Pauls, in Rare Books and Special Collections at Princeton's Firestone Library, for helping me find it; to the Columbia Center for Oral History for providing the transcript of my father's 1976 conversations with Diana Trilling and permitting me to quote from it; to Kirk Curnutt, at the Ernest Hemingway Foundation, for permitting me to quote from Hemingway's 1933 letter to my father; to Gary Shapiro for his assistance in all things Columbia; to Olga M. Nesi, the librarian at Boys and Girls High School in Brooklyn, for combing old Boys High yearbooks for information on my father and my uncle Ed; to Harold Wechsler and Jerome Karabel for their helpful correspondence on Jewish college admissions; to Martin Grams, Jr., for sharing his expertise on *Information Please*; to DorisAnn Kolodny Markowitz for background on her uncle Sidney Franklin; to Rob Sedgwick for refreshing my memories of his delightful family; to Christopher Buckley for showing me that it was not impossible to write a good book about one's father; and to Barry Nalebuff and Reba and Dave Williams for serving me such extraordinary wine that I (almost) loved it.

My understanding of my father's medical issues was aided by Sandy Colt, who answered questions about cancer and end-of-life care; by Sue Li, who tracked down the details of his stay at Mount Sinai Hospital; by Natali Latorre, who provided information about the Bascom Palmer Eye Institute; by Sue Wild, my father's instructor at VIP, who remembered her student and his independent living skills class with fond exactitude; and, especially, by Eve Higginbotham, vice dean and professor of ophthalmology at the University of Pennsylvania's Perelman School of Medicine, who read and improved my descriptions of my father's acute retinal necrosis and its effects on his vision.

I am indebted to two distinguished taste scientists, Virginia Utermohlen and Larry Marks, who invited me to Ithaca and to the John B. Pierce Laboratory at Yale, respectively, for testing and conversation about their fascinating field, after which, along with Dr. Marks's colleague Barry Green, they responded at length and with unfailing good humor to a merciless barrage of e-mails.

Questions of various sorts were graciously fielded by Tom Brown, Timothy Cross, Helen Dunning, Nimal Eames-Scott, J. David Goldin, Lorraine Guimbelot, Laura Johnston, Susannah Lescher, Josh Lieberman, Harrison Monsky, Paul Needham, Gavin Parfit, Bart Paul, Wayne Posey, Allison Primak, Oleg Primak, Bishop Frank Madison Reid III, and Aube Rey Lescure.

Jean-Charles Villeroux and Bryan Martin helped me with French words and phrases; Elisabeth von Stackelberg, Friederike von Stackelberg, Dieter Verdick, and Peter Gradjansky with German; and Maud Gleason with Latin. Two of those advisers are also my dear friends. Peter and Maud not only dispensed linguistic counsel but read parts of the manuscript and provided such useful and sensitive feedback that, *ipsis factis*, I am deeply in their debt.

Three other friends, all of whom I've known for more than two thirds of my life, also gave me loving encouragement. Tina Rathborne listened to me talk about my father, laughed in all the right places, and suggested titles. Jane Condon and Lou Ann Walker always had my back; no matter what happened, they convinced me that

I was writing a terrific book (even though I sometimes thought they might be its only readers).

My father's cousin Fran Cohen; my cousins Jeff, Jim, and Ramsey Fadiman; and my half brother, Jonathan Fadiman, provided background on the Fadimans and, more important, the kind of interest and curiosity that can come only from one's family.

My brother, Kim Fadiman, and I had innumerable conversations about our father at my home in Massachusetts, at his in Wyoming, and on the phone between visits. Without his perspective and his memories, this book would have been duller, thinner, and less accurate. If Kim had wanted to be a writer, he would have been a better one than I. Instead, he is one of the world's best readers—and the one I most want to please. When he told me he thought I'd captured our father, his opinion mattered more than any book review.

I owe my longtime mentor John Bethell an enormous debt of gratitude, both for believing when I was eighteen that I could be a writer and for the support he has given to my writing and editing since then. John helped me choose the photographs for this book and, along with his wife, Helen, the interior and cover fonts.

I will never be able to repay Bill Whitworth for the care he lavished on this book. No one has a better ear. Bill read every sentence more than once, broke my log-jams of indecision by saying Phrase A was better than Phrase B (and Phrase C was better than Phrase D and Phrase Y was better than Phrase Z), and, best of all, talked over those phrases—along with nonrestrictive clauses, pronoun-antecedent agreement, and the glories of parallelism—in long, warm phone calls in which I was constantly reminded that high standards are the only ones worth having. Bighearted friends are the only ones worth having, too.

For research and fact-checking, I am grateful to Rachel Brown, who spelunked heroically through Fadiman family history and genealogy; to Nicolas Niarchos, who checked my early chapters with skill and grace; and, most of all, to my daughter, Susannah Fadiman Colt, who checked the bulk of the book with the patience of a yogi and the acuity of a hawk. (My errors were mice. They didn't stand a chance.) Susannah not only counted the words in Hemingway's spifflicated letter, confirmed that my father had dissed a group of women in flowery hats at a luncheon (not a dinner), and became an expert on Château Lafite Rothschild (and on wine in general), but also made many astute editorial suggestions. Susannah, I wish that Bapa, who dedicated *Worth a Jot* to you not long after you learned to talk, could see what a wordsmith you have become.

My son, Henry Clifton Fadiman Colt, remembers his grandfather less well than his sister does, but he was no less enthusiastic about this project (and when Henry is enthusiastic, it's like being bathed in the light of a 10,000-watt bulb). Thank you, Henry, for noticing when I was discouraged and commanding me to "send it."

My husband, George Howe Colt, kept editing himself out of this book. ("It's not about me," he'd say, and then cross something out with a #2 Ticonderoga pencil.) A few visible vestiges remain, but George, you are invisibly present in every sentence. When I happened upon the WINE MEMORABILIA folder, you listened to me clatter down the kitchen stairs so I could tell you, breathlessly, what I had found. When I decided "the piece about my father and wine" had to be a book, you applauded. When I was tired (and most of the rest of the time, too), you cooked me dinner. When I gave you impenetrable first—and second and third—drafts to read and mark up, you marched fearlessly through the swamp. Writers who marry writers are supposed to fight like cats and dogs, but we just channel our energies into editing each other. What could be better than being able to talk about writing, every single day, with the man I love?

Photo Credits